PUB WALKS
FOR THE FAMILY

Somerset

Charles Whynne-Hammond

COUNTRYSIDE BOOKS
NEWBURY, BERKSHIRE

First Published 1994
© Charles Whynne-Hammond 1994

All rights reserved. No reproduction
permitted without the prior permission
of the publishers:

COUNTRYSIDE BOOKS
3 Catherine Road
Newbury, Berkshire

ISBN 1 85306 306 1

Cover illustration by Colin Doggett
Photographs and maps by Glenys Jones

Produced through MRM Associates Ltd., Reading
Typeset by Paragon Typesetters, Queensferry, Clwyd
Printed in England

Contents

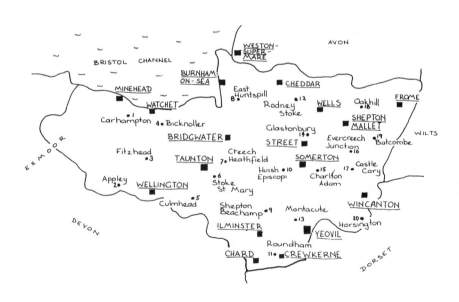

Area map showing locations of the walks.

Introduction

Somerset is perhaps the least-known county in South West England. Cornwall has its rugged coastline and fishing harbours, Devon has its wild, tor-capped moorlands and wooded combes, Dorset has its chalk downs, heathlands and Thomas Hardy connections. But Somerset has fewer 'attractions' that immediately commend themselves to the undiscerning holidaymaker, yet it is one of the prettiest, most varied and quaintest counties in England. Its towns are small, its villages are unspoilt, its hamlets are lost in the folds of the fields. There are hills and moorlands, heather and gorse clad; there are wooded valleys and rugged gorges, sharp with rocky outcrops; there are broad meadows and fenlands, green from floodwaters and alive with wildfowl. Add to all these the legends, myths and mysteries of the county and the mixture becomes almost intoxicating.

Many of the routes described are given shorter or longer options. This will allow readers to design walks to suit themselves, or else to undertake more than one walk from each starting point. There are also suggestions, in the text, for routes or parts of routes, that can be done by those who are pushing prams and wheelchairs. There is no reason why those people with young children, or with disabled friends and relatives, should not be able to enjoy the countryside, and nature, as well as everybody else.

The Ordnance Survey maps referred to in the book are from the 1:50 000 Landranger series. These are invaluable to walkers as they show the features of the landscape, and public rights of way, on a scale most suited to average length walks. All the rights of way should be walkable. Readers who find any difficulty with a public footpath should telephone the local authority, which is responsible for the upkeep of such routes. The telephone number of the Footpaths and Rights of Way department at Somerset County Council is 0823 255657.

Generally, pubs still keep to the traditional opening times – termed 'normal' in the pub profiles. These are 11 am or 11.30 am to 2.30 pm lunchtimes, 6.30 pm or 7 pm to 11 pm evenings. These hours may be extended slightly on Saturdays and reduced slightly on Sundays. Those wishing to eat should aim for the reasonable 'sitting' times, 12 noon to 1.30 pm at lunchtime, 7 pm to 10 pm in the evening. Variations in these times are given in the text, together with the telephone number of each pub, so that prospective customers can check details beforehand. Most of the pubs listed have car parks and allow customers to leave their cars on the premises while going for a walk. However, it is polite to inform landlords before doing so.

All the pubs in this book have facilities for families. Children are welcome inside and out. Most have gardens where play equipment is provided, and most have 'family rooms', or rooms specifically used by families. All are friendly, helpful and comfortable.

Nowadays the choice of food offered is wide, nearly all pubs serving main meals as well as snacks. The pub profiles, of course, do not list every item. They merely give examples of the range and style of the menus concerned. Without exception, all the food provided by these pubs was found to be well cooked and well presented. The drinks offered, also, were wide ranging in choice. Real ale is now served almost everywhere and – this being Somerset – local draught cider is commonly on offer.

Walkers are welcomed at every one of these pubs, but courtesy is advised when wearing wet clothes and muddy boots. Large walking groups should telephone beforehand, if they intend to turn up at a pub 'en masse'. Needless to say, eating one's own food in a pub which serves meals and snacks should not be attempted, except by prior arrangement.

I should like to thank all those pub proprietors who supplied me with valuable information regarding their establishments. I am also indebted to Glenys Jones for taking the photographs and drawing the maps, and to Gwen Cassell who helped with the final draft. I should also like to thank John and Pauline Clark for their 'local' knowledge.

Charles Whynne-Hammond
Summer 1994

Publisher's Note

We hope that you obtain considerable enjoyment from this book; great care has been taken in its preparation. However, changes of landlord and actual closures are sadly not uncommon. Likewise, although at the time of publication all routes followed public rights of way or well-established permitted paths, diversion orders can be made and permissions withdrawn.

We cannot accept responsibility for any inaccuracies, but we are anxious that all details covering both pubs and walks are kept up to date, and would therefore welcome information from readers which would be relevant to future editions.

1° Carhampton
The Butchers Arms

This is a well-known pub and deservedly so. Said to have been, once, a workhouse and, later, an important coaching inn, this Tudor building has cob walls and oak beams made out of ships' timbers. The decor inside has been refurbished but, thankfully, not modernised. The atmosphere is dark and cosy. Horse brasses adorn the bare stone walls and exposed woodwork, and the furniture includes old-fashioned wooden settles.

There is one main bar room, at the front, complete with inglenook and log-burning stove. Two other rooms lead off, almost open-plan yet separated by angles, corners and half-walls. These tend to be used by families. One acts as a dining area, the other contains a pool table as well as dining tables. The garden is at the back, with facilities for children.

As a freehouse the Butchers Arms serves a good selection of beers and ales, ciders and wines, the former including Wadworth 6X and Cotleigh Tawny, the latter including the locally made Rich's farmhouse cider and good value house wine. The selection and quality of food on offer are excellent. The regular menu is listed in a six-page book and includes everything from a light snack to a full blow-out meal. There are ploughman's lunches, sandwiches (both the English and French variety) and jacket potatoes, starters like pâté and soup, and main courses like steak and kidney pies and curries. Vegetarians are offered dishes like pancake rolls and lasagne, whilst various children's menus are available. And, if all this is not enough, daily specials are also written up on the blackboard.

Normal pub opening times are kept, except on Saturdays when the doors are open all day.

Telephone: 0643 821333.

How to get there: Carhampton – pronounced 'Crampton' locally – will be found just 3 miles south-east of Minehead, on the A39 road to Williton. Dunster is the neighbouring village. It is close to the eastern edge of Exmoor National Park. The Butchers Arms stands on the south side of the main road, at the centre of the village.

Parking: The pub has its own car park, opposite, close to the church. Vehicles can also be left in the back streets of Carhampton, provided no obstruction is created.

Length of the walk: 3 miles. OS Landranger map 181 Minehead and Brendon Hills (inn GR 007427).

This is the end of Somerset that is high, wild and spectacular. The Brendon Hills overlook the Bristol Channel, across a narrow coastal plain. To the west are the great heather-clad uplands that are Exmoor. This is walking country par excellence, with clear, well-signposted footpaths and tracks, firm and dry conditions underfoot (even after rainy periods) and wonderful views.

The walk ascends Withycombe Hill, follows its ridge along for a short stretch and then descends, along the edge of Dunster Park. Notwithstanding the steepness of the climb, it is an easy walk and those doing it should take their time fully to enjoy the surroundings. The whole route is along gravelly or stony trackways. There are no faint footpaths to find, no stiles to climb and no thickets to negotiate. Instead there are fine views to enjoy, heather moorlands to admire and dark pine forests to smell.

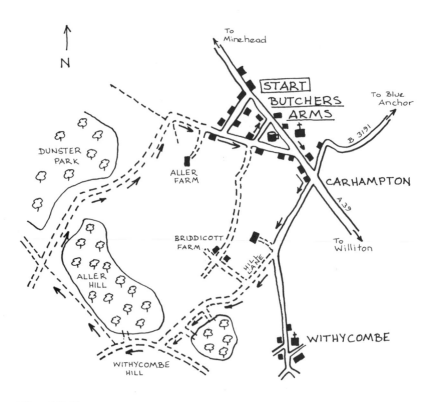

The Walk

Outside the Butchers Arms turn right, to walk up the main road in the Williton direction (south-eastwards). Carhampton church, and the pub car park, should be over to your left. Very shortly the B3191 road to Blue Anchor (and the coast) will be seen leading northwards. Opposite this – that is, on your right – a narrow country lane leads uphill from the main road. This is signposted to Withycombe and marks the start of your country walk.

Those with sufficient time and interest may like to detour before starting their circular route. Carhampton village itself is well worth a second glance, not least because of its old buildings, its quiet corners and its magnificent medieval church. Should you take a short stroll down the B3191 coastwards, you will come to a small hill, commanding fine views all round. It was from the top of this eminence that the artist Turner painted his famous picture of Dunster Castle, which stands just 2 miles away to the west. A little further on, near Blue Anchor, is Marshwood Farm, a 13th century building of great interest and character.

The lane to Withycombe climbs out of Carhampton, leaving the buildings quickly behind. High hedgebanks either side, and tree branches spreading above, make for a fairly dark walk. Soon the lane bears left and two gravel tracks lead off on the right-hand side. Ignoring the first, which goes slightly back and leads to Bowerhayes Kennels, you take the second, going uphill at an angle and called Hill Lane.

This is a lovely little track to follow, with high banks and the cool shade of tall trees. The way it has been worn down into the landscape, making it a 'hollow way', suggests that this route is ancient indeed. It is medieval certainly, and possibly much older – Saxon or even Celtic perhaps. There are many track-ways like this one in the uplands of South West England. Either they evolved as through-routes, linking moorland villages and crossing hill ranges, or else they developed as 'straker ways', along which lowland farmers drove their cattle to upland pastures during summer months.

This particular hollow way is aptly named, for it leads directly to the top of Withycombe Hill. You follow it up all the way. It is a steep climb, in parts, but the stony surface makes it very easy to manage. And numerous stops, to regain your breath, will allow you fully to appreciate the views.

As the gradient of Hill Lane slackens, so you emerge into more open country, with fields either side. In due course, the route bears right and the view spreads out to the right as well as behind. And what a view! Dunster is clear, with its castle on one side and the Conygar Tower rising up above it on the other. Minehead is beyond, the moorland hump of Selworthy Beacon forming the backdrop. Round to your right is Carhampton and the coastal sweep to Watchet. On the far horizon, on clear days, is Wales.

As Hill Lane approaches the summit, the slope becomes more gentle. You reach the pine trees, with a plantation over to your left. Ignoring a couple of tracks that lead into this plantation, you continue up to a gate. Beyond this is the top of your climb.

Now the views are ahead, into the heart of the Brendon Hills.

Dunster Castle.

At the junction of tracks, keep to the right and follow the ridge along. It is a clear, stony path running across a landscape of gorse and bracken. A dry-stone wall, forming the boundary of the plantation, accompanies you on the right, with steep slopes running downhill to your left. The earth here is reddish in colour, making the whole scene beautiful to behold.

Soon the track dips slightly to a farm gate, beyond which it enters the plantation as a wide forest path. Continue onward, ignoring first a rutted track cutting across and then another track forking left. You will see another farm gate ahead – aim for this.

You are now standing at Withycombe Hill Gate, a meeting of trackways at the top of Aller Hill. A footpath signpost stands sentry at this point. Ahead – through the gate – is Dunster Park. To the right is a gravel track running downhill, signposted 'Public Path, Carhampton'. This is the one to follow. And what an attractive walk it provides. On either side is a stone-built earth bank, topped by tall beech trees. After winding around a bit this track narrows and, as you emerge from the woodlands, a view opens out in front. Carhampton lies below, and the sea beyond.

The route back to the Butchers Arms is now simplicity itself. Keep to the gravel track as it continues its descent and turns sharply right. In due course the gravel becomes tarmac and the country track becomes a village lane. Turn left at the second opportunity (at a junction where a small tree forms a mini-roundabout) and continue along High Street. This leads down to the main A39 road. Turn right and the pub is but a few yards away.

Places of interest nearby

Dunster, less than 2 miles away, is a village that really should not be missed. Its medieval High Street, its 17th century yarn market with its octagonal, many-gabled roof, its uniquely powered watermill with twin overshot wheels, its nunnery and its dovecote – all make a gloriously ancient ensemble. At one end is the castle, now owned by the National Trust. This dates from Norman times but was largely remodelled in the 19th century. The gardens are terraced and contain various sub-tropical plants. The tower on top of nearby Conygar Hill is a folly built in 1776.

Minehead, 2 miles beyond Dunster, is a popular holiday resort boasting all the usual tourist attractions. Its Higher Town contains many old buildings, and its railway station is the terminus for the West Somerset Railway.

Washford, 3 miles south-east of Carhampton, is a pleasant little village. The station there has been turned into a railway museum for the old Somerset and Dorset line. It displays models, photos, slide collections, locomotives and wagons. Nearby is *Cleeve Abbey*. This is a remarkably well-preserved Cistercian monastery dating from the 12th century. It is owned by English Heritage, and regularly hosts exhibitions of the monastic way of life.

At Blue Anchor, just 1 mile from Carhampton, is *Home Farm*, situated almost on the beach. It is a working farm where traditional methods and animals are employed. There is also a children's play area and farm quiz.

2 Appley
The Globe Inn

Thought to date back to Tudor times, this pub stands attractively on a hillside along a quiet village lane, surrounded by farmsteads. Inside, all is rustic and comfortable with half-panelled walls and open fireplaces. There is a front entrance, but most customers enter through the back door since this is nearer to the car park. The bar is situated in a passageway at the back.

Children are welcome in the 'Men's Kitchen' one of the two rooms facing the village street. The other is called the 'Magpie Room', owing to its large collection of magpie pictures. There is also a back room, a separate dining-room and, to one side, a skittle alley. Outside is a large garden with a children's climbing frame.

The Globe Inn is a freehouse, serving real ales (Cotleigh Tawny and Kingfisher) and draught ciders (including a local farmhouse brew). The food available is of a very high standard, home-made and freshly prepared. Bar snacks include the traditional ploughman's lunches, soups, rolls and pies and all main dishes are listed on a regular menu. There is always a selection of continental style meals on offer and daily specials – like seafood pancakes and salmon – are listed on a blackboard propped up on the bar. You should not go hungry.

Normal opening times are kept, although the pub closes on Monday lunchtimes, except on bank holidays. The Globe is very popular for its evening meals, served every day from Tuesday to Saturday.

Telephone: 0823 672327.

How to get there: Appley lies 4 miles west of Wellington and 4 miles south of Wiveliscombe. It is close to the Devon border. The village does not stand on a main road. It is most easily reached from the A38 Wellington to Tiverton road, turning north at White Ball and driving through the village of Greenham. The Globe Inn will be found at the northern end of Appley.

Parking: There is a large pub car park. Vehicles can also be parked elsewhere in the village, where the road is wide enough or where lay-bys exist.

Length of the walk: 3 miles. OS Landranger map 181 Minehead and Brendon Hills (inn GR 072215).

Here, we are in the midst of that lovely, unspoilt, hilly region that lies between the Blackdown Hills, to the south, and the Brendon Hills, to the north. The scenery is similar to that more commonly associated with rural Devon – red soils, wooded combes and thatched cottages. This circular walk is to the village of Kittisford and back. Most of the route involves clear footpaths across fields and over stiles. The short sections of road walking are on empty, narrow lanes lined by high hedgebanks.

At one point in the walk there is a glimpse of Cothay Manor, thought by some to be one of the prettiest houses in England.

The Walk

The circuit begins almost opposite the Globe Inn. Slightly downhill, on the other side of the road, is a stile and footpath signpost. Cross into the field and start to enjoy the views.

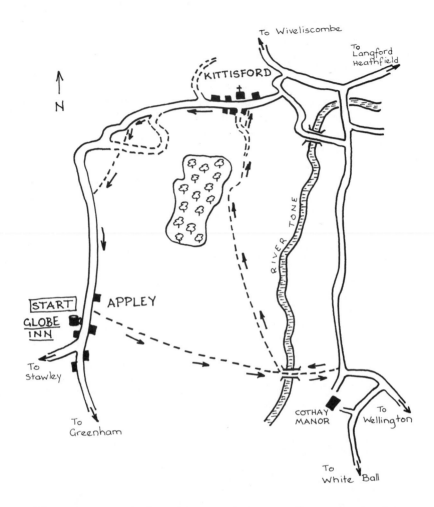

The route to Cothay Manor, about a mile away, is almost straight and very easy to follow, with frequent stiles or gates and numerous arrow discs nailed to them. Down through the first two fields, you keep the hedgerow to your left and the distant view of the Blackdown Hills on the skyline to your right. The Wellington Monument is clearly visible. In due course you reach a signpost pointing left to 'Wood' and straight on to 'River'. Obey the latter and continue straight on (over a stile), still keeping the hedge to your left.

Beyond the next stile/gate you aim slightly right to cross the field diagonally, keeping the large oak tree in the middle to your left. Down in the far corner another stile/gate leads the footpath into a field, across which you keep a small stream to your right. Reaching a small copse of trees, you proceed over yet another stile (next to a metal pedestrian gate) and then go over a little stone bridge. You are now crossing the river Tone which, further downstream, flows through Taunton, to which it has given its name (Tone-tun).

This little spot, on the banks of the Tone and beneath the trees, encourages you to linger – and indeed, it would make an excellent picnic site. Those wishing to see Cothay Manor should proceed along the edge of the next field to reach the road, and then turn right. Those wishing to continue directly with the circular walk can stay a while longer, for the route to Kittisford begins from this point.

Cothay Manor is a large 15th century house with an Elizabethan wing, a crooked porch (probably the oldest part of the building), and a lovely gatehouse which opens onto a broad green. As the road bends round you can obtain different views of the manor, each one as good as the last.

Back at the bridge over the Tone, you re-cross the stile which stands next to the metal pedestrian gate mentioned earlier.

The public right of way from here to Kittisford runs across the field diagonally, to the half right, in the direction of a gap in the far hedge, to the right of a large tree. This takes you into the next field where you turn right and follow the hedge down to a wooden bridge across a stream. Alternatively, you could return over the stile you crossed on your first leg of the journey, and then turn right. In either case you should reach the wooden bridge and cross the stream. On the far side, through a belt of trees, is a barbed wire fence. But fear not. The farmer has kindly wrapped some plastic around the wire rungs – giving much-appreciated protection as you step over.

You are now facing a landscape of large fields, beyond which is a broad sweep of woodland. The public footpath goes to the right of those trees. Cross the first field diagonally, walking under the line of telegraph poles and keeping the wood slightly to the left of straight ahead. As you reach the brow of this gentle hill – for the field rises then falls as it crosses between two shallow valleys – you will see ahead where the route is leading. A clear track goes down over a bridge (there is another stream here) and then up the other side towards Kittisford. Do not, however, follow this track all the way to the village, for it goes through a farmyard. A gate on the right leads to a footpath that crosses a field and then bends left (behind the barns) to reach the road.

The route back to Appley is easy, and very attractive. It is worth making time to go into the church, for it is very old and very beautiful. Everything seems to be made of oak, including the 16th century south arcade and pulpit, dated 1610. There are also brasses showing some of the Bluett family, long-time owners of Cothay Manor.

Leaving Kittisford church behind on your right, follow the lane through the western end of the village and down into a deep combe. As the lane climbs out of the wooded combe, you soon find a stile set into the hedgebank on the left-hand side. A footpath signpost points the way. Walk up over the field, aiming to the right of the trees on the skyline. A wide view now opens out. In the distance, half-left, are the Blackdown Hills, and straight ahead are the green slopes of Devon.

To the right of a group of barns and cattle sheds you cross a stile, a track and another stile. Down across the next field you aim for a metal farm gate in the far corner. There you rejoin the road, turn left, and enjoy the last ¼ mile stretch to Appley and the Globe Inn.

Places of interest nearby

Wellington, 4 miles to the east, grew as a market centre during the Middle Ages, with a successful cloth-making industry. A museum showing the town's history will be found in the old Squirrel Hotel, an 18th century coaching inn. Urban expansion continued in the 19th century with the arrival of the Bridgwater-Tiverton canal and, later, the railway line. Overlooking the town, on the crest of the Blackdowns, is the *Wellington Monument*, built to commemorate the military successes of the Iron Duke, who took his title from the name of the town. From here there are wonderful views all around, and a panorama table to help you identify the distant features.

North-west of Wellington, and 2 miles north-east of Appley,

Cothay Manor.

is the *Langford Heathfield Reserve*, covering 180 acres of lowland heath bounded by ancient oak and ash woodland. A great variety of flora and fauna will be found, such as sallow scrub and wet heathland vegetation, tree pipits, spotted woodpeckers and rare butterflies.

Just a mile south of Appley is *Greenham Weir.* Here there is not only a medieval manor house but also the old course of the canal that once linked Taunton with Tiverton. Across the border into Devon this canal – called the Grand Western – is still a waterway and the area on either side has been designated a Country Park.

3 Fitzhead
The Fitzhead Inn

People come from miles around to enjoy the food and hospitality of this attractive and friendly pub. The evenings, especially, are a popular time as gourmets descend from far afield to enthuse over the chef's prowess. Booking may be advisable. Lunchtimes are quieter but no less pleasant. The mouth-watering menus for both bar food and main meals are written up on a blackboard. Apart from the 'usuals' like ploughman's lunches, sandwiches, steak, gammon, scampi, curry and so on, there are such 'specials' as squid with garlic and chilli, griddled game mix, Mediterranean fish mix, venison sausages and scallops. The chef is especially proud of his seafood dishes, although vegetarians are not forgotten – a Cheddar and walnut savoury looked very good.

The main entrance, leading to both main bars, is down the courtyard, on the left. Children are very welcome and the skittle alley/function room is used for families. All the decor is 'olde worlde' in the nicest sense. There are exposed beams, traditional wooden furniture (much of it hand-made) and cosy log-burning stoves in winter. At the rear of the pub is a gravelled area where tables and chairs are set out, together with a barbecue.

The Fitzhead Inn is a freehouse serving real ales (Cotleigh, Butterknowle and Ushers), a variety of different wines and draught cider. Normal pub opening times are kept.

As an ideal example of a village pub, the Fitzhead Inn should not be missed – especially since the prices are so reasonable. With any change you might have, you could even treat yourself to a coffee or sweet – a chocolate fudge cake perhaps, or passion fruit sorbet.

Telephone: 0823 400667.

How to get there: Fitzhead will be found just 2 miles east of Wiveliscombe and 1½ miles north of Milverton. Taunton is 9 miles away, to the south-east. The village does not stand on a main road. It is most easily reached from the B3227, turning north at the roundabout on the edge of Milverton. The Fitzhead Inn is in the centre of the village.

Parking: There is no pub car park here. Vehicles can, however, be parked anywhere in the village, provided no obstruction is caused.

Length of the walk: 2½ miles. OS Landranger map 181 Minehead and Brendon Hill and map 193 Taunton and Lyme Regis (inn GR 123284).

This is a lovely walk, through a part of Somerset that has not been 'discovered'. The countryside here – the southern edge of the Brendon Hills – is totally unspoilt with little streams running amongst wooded combes and hill pastures patterned with meandering hedgerows. There are views across to the Quantocks and to the Blackdowns.

Apart from a short stretch of footpath, which crosses a single field, the route follows quiet country lanes and clear, deep-set, well-used trackways. The latter are marked as white roads on OS maps and are very common in West Somerset and Devon. They are normally bounded by hedgerows and floored with gravel and earth. This walk has no stiles or fences to climb, and no difficult slopes – so it can be enjoyed by everyone.

The Walk

From the Fitzhead Inn walk downhill to the road junction and turn right. This takes you to the western end of the village. There is an old tithe barn at the corner on your right (in front of the church). This was built to store corn – local tenants giving a tenth of their yields to the parish incumbent in more feudal days – but is now used as a village hall.

At this point turn left, down beside a stone-built house. The gravel roadway runs between two small garages and disappears into a field. You will see a footpath signpost here, labelled 'Beech Tree Cross'. Continue straight ahead.

This is the only footpath to be used on the entire circular walk. Its direction is not difficult to find. Keep to the edge of the field, initially, with the stone wall and hedgerow to your left. Where this hedgerow turns left, cross the field at an angle, continuing in the same direction as before. After just 200 yards you meet another hedgerow, running up from your right. Follow this along to the metal farm gate in the top corner of the field. The route is clear all the way in fact, since the metal gate can be seen across the field, from the point where you leave the first length of hedgerow.

On the far side of the gate you meet a road and turn left. This is a quiet country lane, affording good views to the left towards the Quantocks. Soon you arrive at an off-set road junction. Continue straight on, following the lane signposted to Milverton and Taunton.

In due course, after some undulations in the landscape, you reach a small lane on the right-hand side, with a signpost pointing to Rivers Farm. You take this turning – but you do not go to the farm. Almost immediately a narrow hedged track leads off, again to the right. Unlike the lane to Rivers Farm, which has a firm, gravelly, metalled surface, this track is floored with earth and stones. Take this.

There are many such trackways in Somerset and Devon – narrow lanes that have never been covered in tarmac. They are probably of ancient date – possibly Celtic in origin – and first appeared simply as routeways between farms, or as paths between farmlands and moorlands. They have been worn down with centuries of use, making them, today, 'hollow ways' – tracks sunk into the landscape, winding between earth banks.

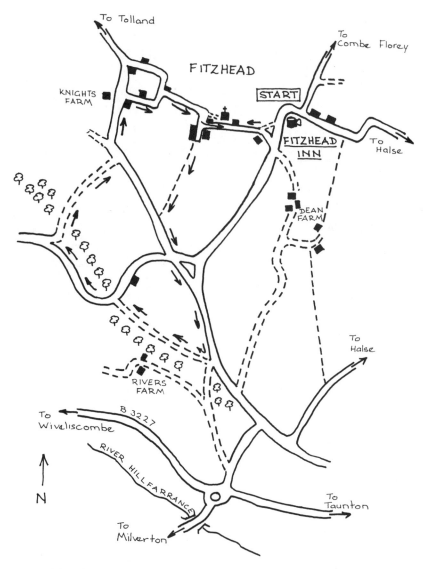

Many, like this one, are now used as bridleways, so the ground underfoot can be churned up, trampled by horses' hooves.

This is a very pleasant part of the walk – dark under the trees, with the hedgebanks on either side thick with ferns and wild flowers in summer. After a while you meet a road and turn

left. This road goes downhill, curving to the right.

Soon the view ahead opens out. Straight ahead, across the valley, is the distinctive shape of Castle Hill, topped by an Iron Age fort. The old ramparts can just be made out in the upper part of the slope. Further away, on the skyline, are the Brendon Hills around Clatworthy.

Continue down the road, ignoring an unfenced track that goes off at an angle on the right-hand side. This merely leads to a house. Shortly after this, and just before the road dips steeper downhill, take the hedged trackway, also to the right. This is another hollow way, similar to the one already taken. This one climbs fairly steeply uphill, at first back and then bearing left. Once again there are high banks on either side and a canopy of trees above. Through the occasional breaks in the hedgerow on the left, there are some fine views towards the Brendons.

Continue uphill. Soon the track levels off and new views open out ahead, this time towards the Quantocks. What lovely countryside this is! Copses and combes, hills and hedgerows with a scattering of farmsteads, hamlets and villages. As the track begins to descend, so the view of Fitzhead village appears, the church nestling in the folds of the landscape. Down at the bottom, the track meets the road and you turn left, to follow the tarmac surface as it rounds a bend to continue the direction you have been following (northwards).

The road walk back to the Fitzhead Inn is now simple. Turn right opposite Knights Farm and follow the road round to a T-junction, where you turn right again. This soon brings you to the tithe barn. You can now retrace your steps through the village.

Places of interest nearby

The little town of *Wiveliscombe* (known locally as 'Wivvy') is an attractive, unassuming place. The buildings mostly date from the 18th and 19th centuries, including the church (which was rebuilt in 1829) and the court house (which is dated 1881). The latter has fine carved wooden wall tiling and is used as a library. In Church Street is the old 'palace' once used by the Bishops of Bath and Wells. Beneath the church are catacombs. These were used during the Second World War to house valuable art treasures, this location being safe from bombing. A plaque lists the items once stored here.

Less than 3 miles east of Fitzhead is *Bishop's Lydeard*. The railway station here stands at the southern end of Britain's longest independent railway line. In summer months steam trains run from here to Minehead.

Gaulden Manor is just 2 miles north of Fitzhead. This dates back to Norman times and is open to the public. It boasts a 17th century hall with a low, highly decorated plaster ceiling. The pretty gardens are especially lovely in springtime.

For those who prefer outdoor activities there is *Clatworthy Reservoir*, 5 miles to the north-west. This has a 6-mile walk around the lake, passing an Iron Age hill fort, and a shorter nature trail, through some ancient woodlands. There is also a car park and picnic site.

Bicknoller
The Bicknoller Inn

This is the archetypal village inn. It is cosy, homely, unpretentious and traditional. Outside, the deep thatch tops the thick whitewashed walls, from which the small windows peer out like half-closed eyes. Inside, all is dark and woody, with red-cushioned settles, bench tables and heavy beams. In one corner there is a stand containing postcards and greetings cards for sale (showing local scenes) and free information leaflets about places to visit nearby. Many of the pictures on the walls show local sports' teams. One shows the Somerset and England cricketer Harold Gimblett (1914–1978) who was born at nearby Blakes Farm. Some of the original paintings, by a local artist, are for sale.

There are two bar rooms, a public bar, where there is a dartboard, and a lounge, where families tend to congregate. Children are welcome. Private parties are catered for, and there is a skittle alley across the yard.

The Bicknoller Inn is a freehouse, keeping normal pub

opening times. The real ales served include Boddingtons and Charrington IPA, and there is a good selection of wines and ciders. Coffee is always available. The menu is compact and you can be sure that everything offered will be home-made and fresh. The usual pub snacks are provided, like ploughman's lunches and sandwiches, and a selection of main dishes is cooked daily. These tend to be traditional and English in character – cottage pie or steak and kidney pie, for instance. There is always something for vegetarians, too.

Telephone: 0984 656234.

How to get there: Bicknoller lies at the foot of the Quantock Hills, below the western slopes at their northern end. The main A358 road from Taunton to Williton runs close by. Taunton itself is 13 miles away to the south-east. Minehead is 10 miles away to the north-west. The Bicknoller Inn stands at the southern end of the village.

Parking: The pub has a very large car park, located opposite, across the road. Vehicles may also be left anywhere else in the village, provided no obstruction is created.

Length of the walk: 2 miles (longer and shorter options). OS Landranger map 181 Minehead and Brendon Hills (inn GR 109393).

There are many walks that can be enjoyed from Bicknoller, both up to the hills and across the meadows which spread out below the village. All local footpaths are well signposted and well trod. The Quantocks rise up steeply to an undulating ridge, covered in heather, bracken and gorse. Deep wooded combes dissect the hill range, producing a most attractive landscape. The meadows, along the bottom of the Doniford Valley, divide the Quantocks from the Brendon Hills. They are well farmed and covered by a patchwork of fields.

This circular walk gives a taste of both hill and meadow landscape. It climbs to a clear path that contours along to an Iron Age settlement (Trendle Ring) and then descends, through a little wooded valley, to return to Bicknoller across a number of pasture fields. It is easy to follow and provides some lovely views across West Somerset.

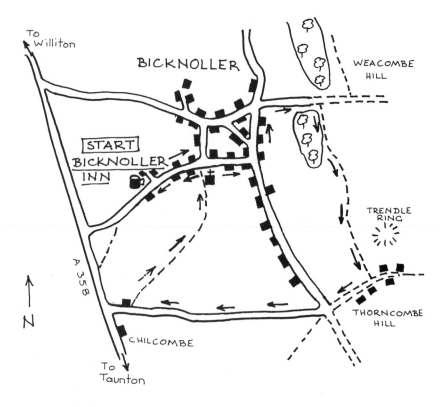

The Walk

From the Bicknoller Inn walk up the lane to the church, passing some attractive red sandstone cottages on the way. The church itself, over to your right, is worth more than a passing glance. It is largely 15th century in date and boasts some fine stone carvings around its walls.

Bicknoller is a lovely little village with many old stone cottages and thatched roofs. Back in medieval times, and earlier, this whole area was heavily wooded, with willows and alders growing on the damp lowlands, oaks and birch trees growing on the dry uplands. Some of this woodland survives, along the deep combes that dissect the hills. The first stretch of the walk follows one of these combes a little way up from the village.

Past the church you reach a junction, where you turn left along Trendle Lane. Keeping to the right at the next fork, you come to a signpost. Turn right at this point, taking the only lane without a directional indicator. This is marked as a 'No Through Road' and is called Hill Lane. Continue up this track – under the trees and along a narrow valley – until you reach a farm gate. Through this you enter National Trust property.

A clear trackway leads on, rising gradually to a slight right bend. Do not follow this. Instead, turn right and take the path which climbs much more steeply, through the trees. Soon this path levels off somewhat and proceeds to contour along the slope. Down to the right, and through the trees, a view begins to appear across to the Brendon Hills.

For the next ½ mile you can enjoy a splendid walk. The footpath is very clear, as it follows the grassy slope along, going up and down with the irregularities of the landscape as it contours its way towards Trendle Ring. Down to the right are the cattle-grazed meadows and, far across the Doniford stream, are the rounded slopes of the Brendons. The tower on top of distant Willett Hill can be seen on the skyline.

In due course you reach a short wooden fence, containing a small gate and a stile. To its left is an old concrete wall with some wire fencing. On the slope above and behind this, is a little derelict hut, of mysterious origin. The route continues through this wooden fence to the path beyond, but Trendle Ring is perched on the grassy ledge above. Those wishing to take a closer look at this ancient site should climb or scramble up through the trees.

Trendle Ring is thought to date back to the Iron Age, making it well over 2,000 years old. It consists of a near-circular enclosure, edged by a bank and ditch. The entrance to this compound can be seen at the eastern end. Archaeologists believe this site was used as a hill fort, consisting of a temporary settlement to which local farmers could retreat in times of war. The name 'Trendle', incidentally, comes from an old word for circle.

The pathway that leads down from the wooden fence, gate and stile leads directly to a lane. You are now at the bottom end of another typical Quantocks' wooded combe. In this one, however, there is a scattering of houses and a farmstead. A foot-path signpost here offers many choices of direction, each one very tempting: Thorncombe Hill, West Quantoxhead, Weacombe.

Those wishing to lengthen their circular walk may like to follow one of these, skirting back down to Bicknoller from the Quantock ridge. Others should proceed down to the right along the lane.

After just 50 yards or so you reach a junction of ways. A muddy track called Thorncombe Lane goes off to the left and the tarmac surfaced Trendle Lane goes off to the right. Anyone who wants to reduce the length of their walk should follow the latter, which leads directly to Bicknoller. A more attractive route back to the village – and the one recommended here – begins down the lane in front. This is called Chilcombe Lane.

Continue down this road, to a point where it bends slightly to the left. Chilcombe Cottage stands on the right. Immediately before this house, you will see a footpath signpost and a farm gate into a field. Go through this gate.

The way back to Bicknoller is now easy. The footpath runs across a number of fields and over several stiles. For most of the way you can see Bicknoller church ahead. The meadows are lush, the grazing animals are tame and the hills look down from all around.

Keeping Chilcombe Cottage to your immediate left-hand side, you continue across the first field to a stile in the far hedge. The little rivulet that flows across the grass, close by that stile, should not cause a problem. Across the next two fields you keep the village church to your half-left. Thereafter you follow the field edge, now with the church directly in front. The road is soon reached. Across all these fields the gates and stiles can be seen from afar, so the direction is easily recognised. Once on the road you will find the church towering above you, and the Bicknoller Inn just a short walk down to the left.

Places of interest nearby

The busy little town of *Williton* is just 2 miles north of Bicknoller and deserves a visit. In Orchard Mill, off Bridge Street, is a museum of country life. The mill itself is 17th century and was opened to the public in 1979 after some restoration. Nearby *Watchet* is an interesting old fishing port where the harbour is still used by local industrial firms. The place is not crowded with tourists and all the better for its lack of holidaymaker facilities.

Bicknoller.

For those who enjoy animal sanctuaries there are two centres to be recommended, *The Bee World and Animal Centre* near Stogumber (1 ½ miles to the south of Bicknoller) and *Tropiquaria* near Washford (3 miles to the north-west). The former is located at the old railway station and shows bee keeping together with collections of ancient farm animal breeds. The latter is located in an old BBC radio station and displays various exotic creatures like snakes, lizards and turtles as well as lemurs, wallabies and kookaburras.

Halsway Manor (1 mile south-east) is a centre for folk dancing and folk music, where visitors are welcome.

Combe Sydenham(3 miles south-west) is a lovely 17th century manor house with medieval and Tudor foundations. The gardens surrounding it include old fishponds, a 'secret valley' and various walks to local viewpoints.

Further afield are *Kilve*, where an old priory, a limekiln and an early 20th century oil retort house overlook the sea, and *Nether Stowey*, where you can visit Coleridge's Cottage, belonging to the National Trust.

⑤ Culmhead
The Holman Clavel

This friendly pub gives a warm welcome to everyone: locals and holidaymakers, passing travellers and walkers. In fact, the place is so welcoming the unfrocked monk who arrived one snowy night is still there. He is the resident ghost. He is harmless, mischievous and called Charlie.

The Holman Clavel is thought to date back to the 14th century. Inside, all is traditional, with low beams and a large inglenook in which an inviting log fire burns during the colder months of the year. There is one main bar, a little side room where the dartboard lives, an extra room, behind, where there is a pool table, and – leading off the latter – a skittle alley. Children are very welcome, families tending to prefer to sit in the quiet games rooms, even though there is no question of having to do so. It is the sort of pub where you can just please yourself.

This is a freehouse, keeping normal pub opening times. The real ales served include Cotleigh Tawny and Butcombe, and barrels of local draught cider may often be discovered behind the bar. The food on offer is excellent and very reasonably priced. Apart from regular bar snacks like ploughman's lunches and sandwiches, you can be tempted by such 'Devon Oak Selection' items as turkey and pork sausages, home-cured ham and smoked salmon. Main hot meals include steaks, fish dishes and pasta. There is a cheese board and good old-fashioned puddings like treacle tart and apple crumble. Live music evenings are held regularly each week and skittles matches are forever filling the pub. It is a convivial place.

Telephone: 0823 421432.

How to get there: Culmhead is not a village as such, but an area where cottages and farms are scattered around. It stands on the northern edge of the Blackdown Hills, surrounded by Forestry Commission woodland. You would hardly guess that Taunton is only 5 miles away to the north, and Wellington only 6 miles away to the north-west. Chard stands 8 miles to the south-east. The Holman Clavel will be found close to where the B3170 crosses the road that runs along the Blackdown ridge.

Parking: There is a car park at the back of the pub and some space for vehicles in front as well. Cars can also be left at the roadside, provided no obstruction is caused. Nearby is a Forestry Commission picnic site with car parking space.

Length of the walk: 3 miles (or shorter option). OS Landranger map 193 Taunton and Lyme Regis (inn GR 222161).

This is an attractive walk with varied scenery. There are woodlands and heathlands, farmlands and scrublands. Views change from expansive panoramas to intimate vistas of deep combes, tumbling streams and thatched cottages. The route is clear throughout, involving paths, bridleways, gravel tracks and country lanes. No difficult terrain is encountered and only a few slopes need be ascended.

Those not wishing to undertake the circuit – and, indeed, those who wish to stay longer at Culmhead – can wander at will through the woodlands opposite the pub. These are run by the Forestry Commission and total access is allowed.

The Walk

Outside the Holman Clavel turn right up to the fork in the road and then bear left, to follow the road signposted to Chard and Staple Fitzpaine. This takes you along under the trees. Very soon you come to another fork, with the principal road bearing right (Chard bound) and a narrow lane going straight on (signposted to Taunton and Corfe). Take the latter, which brings you down to the B3170 main road. To the right is a forested section set aside as a picnic area with car parking spaces. Cross straight over the B3170 onto a footpath. This has a signpost stating 'Staple Fitzpaine 3 miles' and takes a course uphill towards a coniferous plantation.

The walk now becomes very pleasant indeed. At first you are surrounded by tall pines and the rich aroma of their undergrowth but soon the woodland to the left opens out, giving wide views northwards across Taunton. The Quantock Hills can very easily be seen. Even though the line of forest continues on the right, the vegetation underfoot has changed. Now you are walking across upland heath, with bracken, gorse and heather, and the strong smells to match. In due course you reach a gate, with a notice asking you to shut it. It would be polite to do so – but only after you have passed through to the footpath on the other side!

Leaving the woodland behind, you now cross the side of a field, with the hedgebank on your left. Fortunately it is a fairly low hedgebank, so you are still able to enjoy the glorious view over in that direction. Following the field edge along, you soon arrive – at the far corner – at the beginning of another forest plantation (of mixed trees this time). At this point also you join a clear gravel, tractor-rutted track. Continue along this track, roughly in the same direction as before, through a gate and into the trees. For a second time you will see a notice asking you to shut the gate. These woodland areas are run by the Forestry Commission and farm animals need to be kept out.

The forest track goes uphill slightly, for you are approaching the top of Staple Hill – at more than 1,000 ft above sea level, one of the highest points of the Blackdowns. Sadly, there are no views to be had from here, since all around you are tall trees.

As the track descends, but before another gravel track comes up to join it from the left, turn right. The wide footpath that you

34

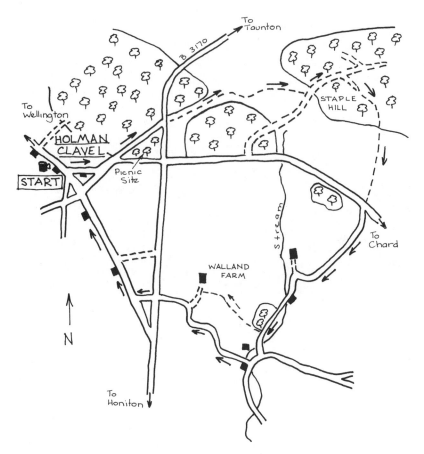

now follow curves up and round, slightly back, and levels off in an area of woodland where many ways seem to join. Straight ahead you will see a wooden farm gate. Approach this but do not go through it. Just before you reach the gate turn right, along a wide wooded avenue. About 40 ft wide and hemmed in by earthen banks surmounted by a hedge and trees, this is a very pretty stretch. It is also, probably, very old. It looks as though it could well have been part of a medieval forest way – connecting Staple Fitzpaine with Otterford perhaps.

After a couple of hundred yards along this wide trackway you reach the edge of the wood. In front is a gate, a field and, beyond, a fine view to the south-west, over the Blackdowns as they sweep into Devon.

Farmland around Culmhead.

Go through the gate and walk diagonally across the field, aiming for the view. Very soon you reach a fence. Bear right and follow this fence down, keeping it to your left. At the bottom of the hill you will reach a gate onto the road. Should you wish, you could turn right, along the road, in order to go back to the Holman Clavel. But this would not only cut short the circular walk, but would also deprive you of some very pretty scenery still to come.

The remainder of the circular route is, in fact, along quiet country lanes, with old tarmac surfaces. The hedgerows are alive with flowers and the views across the hills are lovely.

From the gate cross straight over, and take the narrow lane ahead that leads past a couple of cottages and downhill. After crossing a small stream and bearing right, this lane continues, eventually running down into a valley and following a little river along. The river is one of the upper tributaries of the river Yarty, which flows southwards into Devon to meet the river Axe near Axminster.

This is a beautiful walk, along the bottom of a wooded combe and beside a tumbling brook. Beyond a stone cottage, which

36

stands on the left, the lane passes a larger patch of woodland on the right. It then bears left over a ford. At this point a choice of routes presents itself.

The easier route lies along the lane you have been following. This takes you up to a T-junction where you turn right, go down to the river again, turn right by a cottage and up the lane out of the valley, continuing until you reach the B3170.

The harder route – although very clear – takes you up to the right, along a footpath under the trees (near a derelict building) and thence up across fields to Walland Farm. There you follow the farm track back to the lane and turn right to reach the B3170.

At the 'B' road, cross straight over to another lane and then turn right at the next T-junction. This takes you back to the Holman Clavel.

Places of interest nearby

Very close to the Holman Clavel and, in fact, signposted at the adjoining crossroads, are the *Widcombe Bird Gardens*. Here, amongst a pretty parkland where rhododendrons and azaleas flourish, are collections of tamed animals – llamas deer, donkeys and Shetland ponies – and a variety of birds.

Just 3 miles to the east is *Castle Neroche*. Here are the remnants of a Norman castle, its central motte and surrounding ramparts still very visible. Castle Neroche Farm occupies part of the site and contains some of the castle's old stonework. From here wide views can be enjoyed. The area is also surrounded by Forestry Commission woodland, with a forest trail, a car park and picnic area.

At *Poundisford Park* (2½ miles north of the Holman Clavel) is a lovely Tudor manor house, surrounded by simple yet pretty gardens. Inside are some fine 16th century plaster ceilings and a small exhibition of 18th and 19th century costumes. In the park is an unusual 17th century summer-house.

The famous *Wellington Monument*, standing on the top of the Blackdowns overlooking Taunton Deane, is 5 miles away to the west. The views from here are splendid.

6 Stoke St Mary
The Half Moon Inn

This is a handsome Victorian/Edwardian pub, standing side-on to the village street. Inside it is extremely spacious, with various bars and lounges interconnected, not quite open-plan since spindle screens help divide up the sitting areas. There are separate dining-rooms and plenty of space where families can spread out. Children are welcome in this comfortable and friendly pub. The decor is modern but traditional, with some exposed brick walls, wood-panelling and numerous old prints hung about. The floor is carpeted and furniture is of the wooden settle variety.

The Half Moon Inn is a Whitbread house, serving real ale (including Wadworth and Boddingtons), draught cider and a whole host of country fruit wines. All the food is fresh, home-cooked and delicious, and there should be no complaints about the choice. From basic snacks upwards there is something for everyone, including vegetarians and unadventurous children. There are sandwiches, soups, cheese-based lunches and jacket potatoes with various fillings, as well as specials such as stuffed aubergines, tagliatelle, grilled lamb chops or baked ham. There is also a set 'Lunch and Early Evening Dinner' which gives a choice of four items in each course – starters like seafood crêpe and fried potato wedges, main courses like lasagne and chicken/ham/leek pie, desserts like ice-cream and apple pie.

The pub keeps normal opening times. There is a pleasant garden and a large patio area with tables and chairs.

Telephone: 0823 442271.

How to get there: Stoke St Mary is 2½ miles from the centre of Taunton. It is just south of the A358 road to Ilminster, almost a stone's throw from the M5 motorway. The Half Moon Inn stands in the centre of the village, west of the church.

Parking: There is a large pub car park at the back. Vehicles can also be left along the village street, provided there is enough space for passing traffic.

Length of the walk: 3 miles (or shorter options). OS Landranger map 193 Taunton and Lyme Regis (inn GR 264223).

This walk crosses the pleasant, undulating countryside south-east of Taunton, where the hills of south Somerset merge with the meadows of the river Tone. After a wooded ascent of Stoke Hill, the route circles the village of Stoke St Mary via Henlade. There are extensive views to be enjoyed, towards the Blackdowns and across to Glastonbury and the Mendips.

Much of the circuit involves footpaths that go over farmland, skirting fields and crossing several stiles. After periods of rainfall some stretches are also liable to be wet underfoot, so strong footwear is recommended. All the paths are clearly marked, either by being well used or by being well signposted.

The Walk

Outside the Half Moon Inn turn right and walk eastwards through the village, up to the church. At this point the road bends left and a rough, but wide, track continues straight on, running between the church and a thatched cottage. Follow this until you reach an entrance gateway, upon which is written 'Private. Stoke House and Stoke Cottage'. Ahead lies a gravel drive, running beneath the trees to bend right and out of sight.

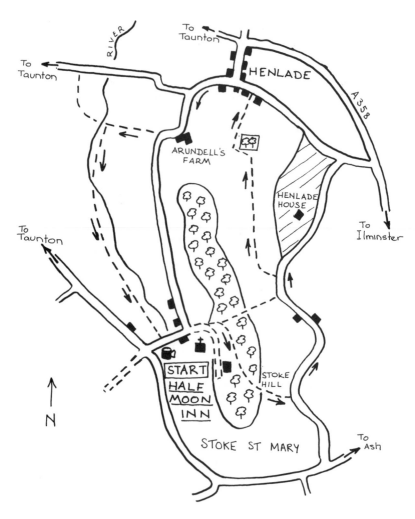

Do not be alarmed. There is a public right of way here. It is not signposted but is very clear. It will be found to the left of the left-hand gatepost. A well-marked footpath continues parallel to the driveway, but going uphill slightly more steeply. There is a hedge to the left. As the driveway, now below you to the right, makes its turn to the right, so does the footpath, gaining height all the time.

Unless you wish to reduce the total length of the circular

route by ½ mile, ignore the steep footpath that you will see going up to the left. This bypasses the top of Stoke Hill. The route you want continues uphill more gradually. This is easier to walk along and gives better views.

After an early dip, where the path goes down then up again, this route is consistently rising through the trees. In fact, it is a very pleasant stretch, with pretty woodlands either side and – over to the right and through the trees – glimpses of a view towards the Blackdown Hills. After a period of prolonged wet weather the ground underfoot is liable to be muddy as this footpath acts as a channel down which the water of the hillside drains.

Towards the top – for you are, in fact, walking over Stoke Hill – the footpath bears left and widens out, to run between two old hedgebanks. Could this be a remnant of an ancient trackway? Could it be an ancient boundary line with the earth bank on each side marking the edge of some medieval farm? Perhaps. But today it gives a most attractive stretch of footpath.

Soon you reach a tarmac road – a small country lane that has very little traffic. Turn left. Now the views northwards open up before you. The Mendips are straight ahead and, round to the right, Glastonbury Tor rises up from the Levels. On a clear day the prospect is glorious.

The lane leads you downhill, winding around a little and passing, first, a farm and then the appropriately named Mendip View Nurseries. In due course the slope downhill steepens and the lane veers to the right. A gate then presents itself on your left, together with a stile and public footpath signpost. These lead you to a wide track between hedges which, after about 100 yards, bends to the right and ends. And there, on your right, is another gate, complete with arrow disc directing the way. On the skyline ahead, over Taunton, are the Quantock Hills.

The route now makes its way downhill, across farmland, to the village of Henlade, which you can see below. The path follows the edge of two fields, in each of which you keep the hedge to your right. There is a stile between the two fields. At the bottom of the second you turn left and right (keeping within the same field) in order to go round two sides of a little orchard. Beyond the next stile you go straight across the field, through the middle aiming for the left-hand side of a bungalow. After a

Stoke St Mary.

further stile the path leads you through a small thicket, around the back of a house, and on to the road. This is Henlade. Turn left.

You now keep to the tarmac lane for about ½ mile, ignoring the first turning to the right and then, after the next bend, taking the left option, signposted to Stoke St Mary. This brings you up to Arundell's Farm where the road bends right. Shortly after this you come to a sharp left bend.

A choice now presents itself. The easier and shorter way back to the Half Moon Inn is simply along the road that leads directly to Stoke St Mary. The longer and prettier way – but one that could be slightly damp underfoot after wet weather – is across the fields. The latter is, of course, the one to be recommended.

Instead of turning left up the road, continue straight on through the gate where a footpath signpost points the direction. Keeping to the hedgerow (on your right), you now walk along the edges of two fields, going through another gate on the way. At the far corner of the second field you will find a little wooden bridge crossing a stream, leading to a track that goes past a Dutch barn. Do not take this. Instead, turn left and keep within the field you have just crossed. The hedge, and the stream, should be on your right. Up in the next corner a small bridge, made of concrete planks with a metal rail, takes you across the stream you have been following.

The route to Stoke St Mary is now easy. You keep the stream immediately to your left and walk along the edges of two meadow fields, crossing a fence and ditch to reach the second from the first. This second field narrows. In the far corner another concrete plank bridge, complete with metal rail, takes you to a narrow path. There is an old bench seat here.

Continue along this narrow path, keeping the wire fence to your right. Do not be tempted to follow any of the alternative paths leading off to the left. These go to other parts of the village. The path you want – along the wire fence – leads straight on, eventually coming out to the road next to a thatched cottage. The Half Moon Inn is now almost opposite.

Places of interest nearby

Hatch Court, which is situated outside Hatch Beauchamp, 3 miles to the south-east, is a Palladian style mansion dating from 1755. Inside there is a China Room and a Canadian Regimental Museum. Outside is a deer park. The elegant Orangery and the curved screen, which act as wings to the mansion, were built in 1800.

The nearby village of *Curry Mallet*, east of Hatch Court, is almost entirely owned by the Duchy of Cornwall. It has an attractive medieval church where, each January, a traditional service is held, the Blessing of the Plough.

Just 3 miles south-west of Stoke St Mary is *Poundisford Park*. This is a Tudor house with a display of costumes dating from the 18th and 19th centuries and, in the garden, a 17th century summer-house.

Creech Heathfield
The Crown Inn

Curiously, this pub is known locally as the 'Drum and Monkey'. It is said that, years ago, a busker used to frequent the village, playing his drum and using his pet monkey to collect up the pennies thrown by kindly passers-by. And with his musical earnings the busker would enjoy a pint or two at his favourite alehouse.

Today the Crown is still a favourite alehouse, patronised by locals, by Taunton folk who come here specially, by holidaymakers and by walkers. In fact, the pub is appreciated by all who like an unpretentious village tavern where good food and beer are served in simple, comfortable surroundings and a friendly atmosphere. Children are welcome, inside as well as out. There are two main bar rooms, a public bar where locals and drinkers tend to congregate and a lounge/dining-room where families tend to sit, and those others who want more of a quiet, smoke-free atmosphere. There is also a skittle alley at the back. The decor may be described as 'old rustic', with lots of wood, beams, bare stone walls and a large inglenook. Open fires burn in the winter months, further enhancing the warmth of the reception all customers are given.

Various real ales are served, including Cotleigh Tawny and Courage Best, and the range of wines and liqueurs offered would not be out of place in a restaurant or wine bar. All the food is freshly made and home-cooked. The Crown specialises in wholesome pub cooking, large portions and no-nonsense menus. All kinds of snacks are available – sandwiches, jacket potatoes and ploughman's lunches, for instance – together with such traditional fare as steak and kidney pie and fisherman's pie. There are curries and lasagne, and always something for vegetarians. The omelettes are excellent. Normal pub opening times are kept.

Telephone: 0823 412444.

How to get there: Creech Heathfield is not far from the eastern outskirts of Taunton, close to the M5 motorway. It can most easily be reached from the A361 Taunton to Glastonbury road. From the A358 Taunton to Chard road it can be found on the far side of Creech St Michael. A little to the north of Creech Heathfield are the lower slopes of the Quantock Hills. The Crown Inn stands on the eastern side of the main village street, approached up a narrow lane.

Parking: There is a large pub car park. Vehicles can also be left along the village lanes, where space permits. There is not much passing traffic.

Length of the walk: 2½ miles (or longer options). OS Landranger map 193 Taunton and Lyme Regis (inn GR 278273).

Somerset is not famous for its canals. The few that were built during the Industrial Revolution were not gloriously successful. Many were short-lived and fell into decay – like those near Westport and Wellington. But one canal has survived intact – the Bridgwater and Taunton canal. This walk includes a stretch along that canal, following the towpath for about a mile.

To reach the canal, footpaths are used which cross fields and involve some stiles. The return journey is a simple stroll along a country lane which, because it is a dead-end, has almost no traffic. Throughout, the route is clearly marked and the ground underfoot is firm.

The Walk

The route begins immediately from the Crown Inn car park. A grass path leads south, along the side of the car park, away from the pub. After winding around a little, next to some cottages and garages, this path reaches a tarmac lane, with some bungalows opposite. Turn right and walk about 50 yards, to where you will see a 'Public Footpath' signpost over on the left-hand side of the road. Follow the direction indicated, down a track called Meads Droveway. Do not go down the adjacent lane, called Francis Close, which merely leads to some houses.

Meads Droveway takes you down to an apparent dead-end, with a house called Sunny Dale in front. Fear not, for a narrow pathway continues. This leads off to the right, along by a hedge, and curves around the house. It then continues between a stone wall and a hedge. At the far end a track runs off to the right but you continue straight on to a stile. This takes you on to the open fields.

The route onwards is quite clear, the path across the grass being well used and the arrow discs, nailed upon the occasional stile, confirming the direction. You walk along the edges of two fields, keeping the hedgerow to your left each time, and then proceed (in the same direction) up a wider path that runs, between hedges, to a gravel track. All along this stretch the Blackdown Hills are over to your half-right, giving an attractive skyline of slopes and trees.

Turn right down the gravel track, which bends around a farmyard and meets a junction of ways. At this point you take the lane marked, by a road sign, as a dead-end. This runs south, to continue the direction you have been following since Creech Heathfield. Do not – unless you intend having a longer circular walk and, in so doing, seeing the village of Creech St Michael – take the gravel track that leads right, past some houses and garages.

The lane running south is marked as a dead-end because it goes down to the canal, and not beyond. You follow it all the way. It has a firm surface – stones and old metalling – and therefore makes for an easy walk. At the second cottage you pass, down towards the bottom end, you will notice a footpath coming in from the right-hand side (over a field) and going off to the left-hand side (along by the house). You could turn left

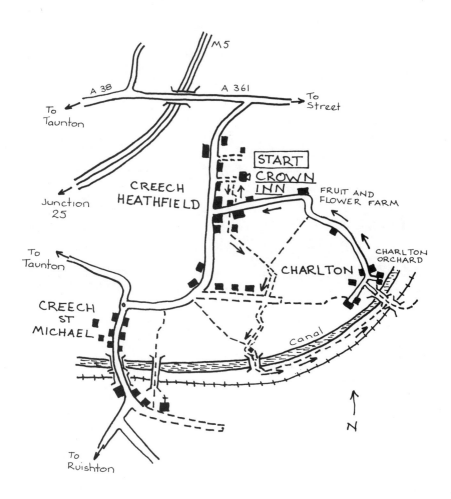

here if you wish, but this only cuts off a bend in the track. It is easier simply to stay on the lane, which bends left, then right until it reaches the canal. Cross the bridge and turn left along the towpath.

The Bridgwater and Taunton canal was opened in 1827. It was intended to link Somerset's county town with the Bristol Channel, thus to encourage Taunton's trade and industry. Some little success resulted and Taunton gained some wharf facilities. But the railways soon came and took all business away from the narrow boats and barges. The main line through

47

The Bridgwater and Taunton canal.

Taunton opened in 1842 and, thereafter, the canal fell into disuse. Today it is used, largely, as a relief drainage channel for the Somerset Levels.

The walk along the towpath is very pleasant, with meadows on either side and the distant Somerton Hills over to the right. On one side are the quiet waters of the canal, on the other the main railway line, with its occasional Inter-city express. Apart from the wildlife, you should notice the sad remnants of the recent past. As well as the semi-dilapidated railway building there are wartime pillboxes, now almost lost under weeds. These, of course, were built to protect the railway and canal from Nazi attack, during the dark days of the 1940s.

The fields over to the left, across the canal, have been turned into a golf course and the area is landscaped with trees and small hillocks. In due course, along the towpath, you reach the canalside hamlet of Charlton. Cross over the old canal bridge and, keeping to the right, follow the country lane that leads past Charlton Orchard. This stands on the right-hand side and is open to the public in season.

This last stretch – along the lane that cuts through the golf course and past a fruit and flower farm – is quiet and pleasurable. The hedgerow either side is low enough to afford a view across the countryside and there is much bird life to distract your attention. Eventually you arrive back at Creech Heathfield. At the edge of the village turn right just after the thatched house called Salters and alongside the cottage called South View. This is the path you took at the very start of the walk. It bends round past some garages and leads back to the Crown Inn car park.

Places of interest nearby

Maunsel House, which stands 2 miles away north-east of Creech Heathfield, close to North Newton, is a small manor house dating from the 15th century. Its Great Hall is a fine example of medieval workmanship.

Hestercombe House, 2½ miles away to the north-west, is not open to the public but its gardens are. These were laid out in the early 20th century by Sir Edward Lutyens and Gertrude Jekyll. The Orangery is much admired and the raised pathways offer good views over Taunton.

Close to Stoke St Gregory (4 miles east of Creech Heathfield) is the *English Basket Centre*. Demonstrations are offered there of the traditional skills involved in turning willow wood into household goods. Also nearby, is the *Willows and Wetlands Visitor Centre*. Here too the craft of willow-working is practised and explained.

East Huntspill
The Bason Bridge Inn

East Huntspill is a strange, interesting place. Working farms stand cheek-by-jowl with commercial units, fields are edged with isolated bungalows; and modern residential streets fill up the gaps between old cottages. It is a village with the feel of a town, an agricultural area with the smell of industry. Indeed, smell is the operative word, for there is a large food processing plant here and the air is frequently heavy with the sweet aromas of fruit or dairy products.

The Bason Bridge Inn successfully captures the mixed atmosphere of East Huntspill. It has the feel of a town pub but the decor of a country one. The furnishings are plain and simple but the decorations – the pictures and bar surround – are rustic. In fact, it is an extremely pleasant, cosy, comfortable pub with a very happy atmosphere. Everyone, including children, are made to feel very welcome. There is one main bar room, but this is laid out in such a way that different sections feel like separate rooms. At one end is the pool table and dartboard, and the other end – in a large alcove – is a space resembling a dining area. The pub also possesses a large function room and an unusual double skittle alley.

Open during normal pub times, this freehouse serves various real ales (including Boddingtons and Flowers IPA) and an interesting selection of spirits and mixes (like shrub and lovage). An extensive menu lists a wonderful variety of snacks and main meals. From toasted sandwiches, king-size rolls and burgers, the selection rises through curries, lasagne and fish dishes to the chef's specials, like steak and kidney pie. There are children's menus and vegetarian meals, like broccoli and cheese bake. Portions are large and all the food is freshly made.

Telephone: 0278 782616.

How to get there: East Huntspill lies east of the Parrett Estuary, where the flat meadows of the Somerset Levels meet the Bristol Channel. Highbridge and Burnham-on-Sea are just a few miles away, Weston-super-Mare is 10 miles to the north and Bridgwater 6 miles to the south-west. Bason Bridge is the name of the northern end of East Huntspill, where the B3141 road crosses the river Brue. The inn stands on the eastern side of that main road. It can be reached easily from junction 22 of the M5 motorway.

Parking: There is a large pub car park. Both the main road through the village, and the side turnings, also offer space for vehicles to be left.

Length of the walk: 2½ miles. OS Landranger map 182 Weston-super-Mare and Bridgwater (inn GR 347459).

The countryside here recalls the Fen country of eastern England. It is a landscape of broad skies and wide horizons, of flat fields and drainage ditches, of distant trees and cottages standing up above the skyline. This is an area enjoyed by both anglers and bird-watchers because it is alive with fish and wildfowl.

This route follows the south bank of the river Brue downstream and then takes a course over a sluice bridge to return by way of a clear gravel farm track. The outward journey involves a footpath across a series of fields. Many stiles must be climbed, and a few plank bridges over ditches must be crossed. It is a pleasant little walk, especially for those interested in wildlife.

The Walk

From the Bason Bridge Inn walk down the B3141 southwards. The Brue Business Park will be seen on the left. You cross the bridge over the river Brue itself and immediately, on the right, you will see a stile (before the first house on that side of the road). This marks the beginning of the footpath along the river-bank and, therefore, the beginning of your circular walk.

For the next mile or so you keep close to the river, which flows in the direction you are walking. To your left are the flat fields of the Somerset Levels. There are many fields to cross, and many stiles, but the route is extremely clear. Each stile can be seen from the previous one. All the way you should keep an eye out for the bird-life. Ducks, moorhens and herons are common in these parts and cormorants may well come in from the sea. The trees and hedgerows are alive with song birds.

The Somerset Levels were once much wetter than they are today. The hills and knolls that rise up from their meadows – like Brent Knoll, which can be seen clearly throughout this walk – were more like islands. Distant Glastonbury is thought to have been the fabled Isle of Avalon. Drainage began in medieval times, at first in a piecemeal fashion and organised by the great monasteries of the region like Muchelney and Athelney. But later, in Tudor times, reclamation became more systematic, financed by local landowners. By the end of the 18th century drainage was almost complete. Acts of Parliament had allowed the enclosure of the farmland and the Levels had taken on their present appearance.

Today the Levels – called Moors locally – have a distinctive character. Pollarded willow trees line the drainage ditches (called 'rhynes', pronounced 'reens') and winter floods fill the old peat diggings.

Soon after leaving the road, at the start of your walk, you will notice an old brick cottage on the far side of the river, and a derelict wartime pillbox. These act as reminders of the railway line that once ran along the north bank of the river Brue. This was the northern end of the Somerset and Dorset Railway. Its southern end ran to Poole. Originally the 'S and D' was built with the intention of linking Wales to France, connecting up with ferries from Cardiff and to Cherbourg respectively. But it was never a great success. It closed in the 1960s, mourned and

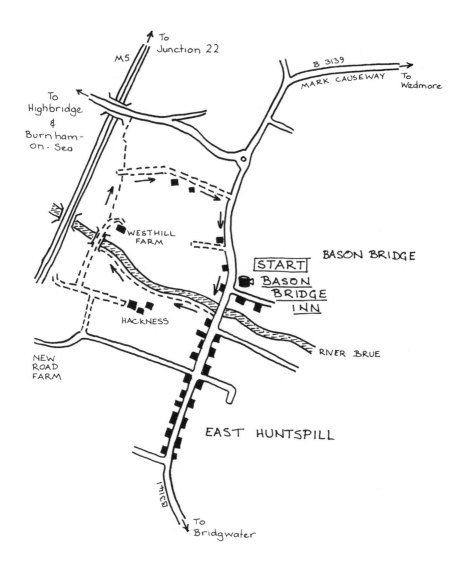

To Junction 22

M5

B 3139

MARK CAUSEWAY

To Wedmore

To Highbridge & Burnham-on-Sea

WESTHILL FARM

BASON BRIDGE

START

BASON BRIDGE INN

RIVER BRUE

HACKNESS

NEW ROAD FARM

EAST HUNTSPILL

B3141

To Bridgwater

missed by many a railway enthusiast.

A little further along, after you have crossed several stiles and footbridges, you pass close to a farmstead (to your left). Here and there, in the fields, you will see a few gnarled old fruit trees. These are the last remnants of an orchard. Years ago, nearly every Somerset farm had its own orchard – and from its own apples made its own cider. Some farms even made their own 'calvados' or apple brandy, illegally of course. Ah, happy days!

In due course you arrive at Hackness Sluice, where a bridge carries a trackway across the Brue. On the far side is a mobile home site, a caravan park used by holidaymakers. Nestling close by is another wartime pillbox, a further reminder of the lost railway. Beside the track, as it crosses the bridge, is an information board. This tells visitors all about the Levels – the farming, fishing and wildlife of the area, the wetland habitats and the future plans regarding conservation and flooding schemes. The board also tells the story of elvers and eels, which commonly live in these channels. There is even a recipe for elver pie. From Hackness Bridge, traffic on the M5 motorway can be seen, and heard, across the fields. Fortunately this does not disturb the peace too much.

The route takes you across the bridge and past the entrance to Westhill Farm and Caravan Park. In front is a good view of Brent Knoll in the distance. Where the track swings right, into Westhill Farm, you continue straight on, along a clear grassy path that runs between two lines of tall trees and bushes. Technically, the right of way runs alongside this pathway, to its left, but the variation is academic. Within 100 yards you reach a T-junction, with a wide farm track running across from left to right. Turn right.

This track is, in fact, the western end of Westhill Lane. It runs as a long, straight, tractor-rutted path, bounded by hedgerows some 10 yards apart. At first the surface is earthy, but this later changes to firmer gravel. Beyond Ash Tree Farm the track becomes a tarmac lane and, further on, passes by some bungalows on the right. Immediately to the left is a deep rhyne, beyond which are the open fields.

At the main road (the B3141) turn right. East Huntspill soon appears in front and it does not take long, walking along the pavement conveniently provided, to arrive back at the Bason Bridge Inn.

Places of interest nearby

New Road Farm, just 1 mile away at Hackness, advertises a fascinating 'Secret World of Somerset Wildlife'. It is a working farm and visitor centre where orphaned and injured animals are protected, farming demonstrations are given and 'hands-on' exhibitions are organised. Badgers and foxes can be seen – there is a specially built nocturnal house – together with some unusual farm animal breeds. Visitors are free to explore the site and children are given their own play area and farm trail. There is also a gift shop and tearoom.

At Westhay, 6 miles south-east of East Huntspill, there are three places where you can find out more about the life and history of the Somerset Levels. The *Peat Moors Visitor Centre* gives a visual interpretation of the area, its archaeology, flora, fauna and industrial history. There are replicas of Iron Age houses and trackways, a garden centre and tearoom. Nearby, the *Shapwick Heath National Nature Reserve* protects rare dragonflies and marsh flowers, and the *Westhay Moor Nature Reserve* preserves some derelict peat workings.

Along Mark Causeway, just 2 miles north of East Huntspill, is the *Coombes Cider Farm and Museum* where cider making is demonstrated and explained. You can also taste and buy the product. A little further north from here is *Chapel Allerton* where a fully restored and working windmill can be visited.

9 Shepton Beauchamp
The Duke of York

The internal dimensions may surprise you. From outside, the Duke of York looks like an ordinary village pub, of normal size and offering, say, two main bars. Inside, however, there are rooms everywhere, with lots of space for diners, drinkers, locals and families. And the welcome is warm and friendly too. At the front, the public and saloon bars are interconnected. Open fires burn all winter, and wall lights glow above the traditional wooden furniture. To one side, around a corner, a further room offers space away from the bar and, at the back, another large room acts as a restaurant. Up a short corridor is a very pleasant conservatory, beyond which is the beer garden.

The Duke of York is a freehouse and keeps normal pub opening times. The real ales served include Hancock's, and cider can be bought on draught, but it is the food served which makes this a particularly popular and inviting establishment. The main offerings are chalked up on the blackboard over the fireplace – and the choice is tempting in its variety and quality. All is freshly made, home-cooked and very reasonably priced. From simple snacks like sandwiches and ploughman's lunches the menu rises up through curries, chillies, burgers and lasagne to the more traditionally English pie dishes – fisherman's, steak and kidney and so on. There are lots of 'things' with chips so the children should be happy as well. No wonder so many people eat at the Duke of York.

Telephone: 0460 240314.

How to get there: Shepton Beauchamp nestles at the southern edge of the Somerset Levels, where the flat meadows begin to merge with the Hamstone Hills. Ilminster is just 3 miles away to the south-west. Yeovil is 10 miles to the east, Taunton is 12 miles to the north-west. The village is most easily reached from the A303, via South Petherton. The Duke of York stands at the northern end of the village.

Parking: There is a large pub car park, situated at the back. Vehicles can also be left, where space permits, along the village streets.

Length of the walk: 3 miles (shorter and longer options). OS Landranger map 193 Taunton and Lyme Regis (inn GR 403173).

This route incorporates the villages of Barrington and Stocklinch. It involves some footpath-walking across fields and some climbing of stiles. There are also stretches of bridleway, along which horses' hooves may have churned up the ground underfoot. The lanes used, though metalled, are generally traffic-free. There are few slopes and the effort required is minimal. Throughout the circuit there is plenty to see, from the wildlife in the hedgerows to the views across south Somerset.

The Walk

The route begins along the side of the Duke of York, where a sign points the way to the pub car park. But – with time permitting – you should really look round the village first. It is an attractive, bustling little place with many old stone cottages, a few shops and a medieval church which boasts one of the most beautiful towers in Somerset. Those with prams or wheelchairs to push would certainly enjoy taking a circular

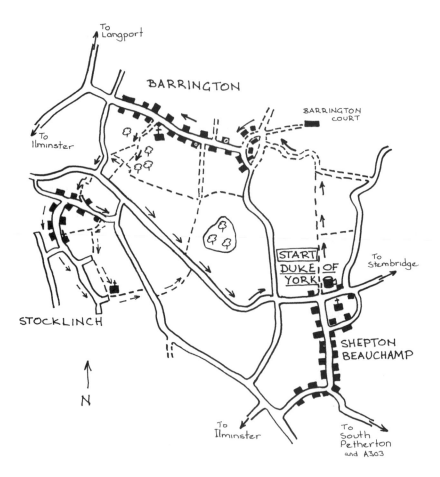

stroll, down through the main street of the village to the southernmost end, then turning right and right again along a country lane back to the junction westwards of the Duke of York. Here turn right again, thus completing a large, rectangular 'block' a little over one mile in distance.

On the eastern side of the main street, south of the church, you will see a fives wall. This is one of five such walls in south Somerset, the others being at Stoke sub Hamdon, South Petherton, Martock and Hinton St George. Fives was a popular game during the 18th century. It resembled squash except that the players used their hands instead of rackets. 'Somerset Fives' was a particular version of this game and resembled the Spanish game of pelota. The pupils of Sherborne School in Dorset still play it.

Back at the Duke of York the track you want is marked by a wooden post, indicating a footpath to Barrington Court and Shells Lane. It runs beneath the trees, past the pub car park on the right, and on to a rough flight of steps leading up to a stile. Beyond this are the open fields.

The route is very easy to follow. It goes almost dead straight across a number of fields and a series of stiles. Each of the stiles has a footpath arrow disc, pointing the way ahead. All the while, you keep the hedgerow or fence to your right and every field you cross to your left, that is, you keep to the field edges all the way. The path rises to a brow of a gentle hill and then runs down to Barrington. All around are views across the green undulations of south Somerset – the Somerton Hills ahead, the slopes up to Windwhistle behind. Down across the valley in front is Barrington Court.

Soon you meet a gravel trackway, which you follow onwards. This leads you down to a left bend, after which you enter a small group of trees. In due course you meet a T-junction. You can go either way, since both right and left will take you to the southern end of Barrington village. Turning right will bring you to the entrance to Barrington Court, where the track swings round to pass some handsome stone buildings.

Barrington is a delightful village, with a plethora of yellow Hamstone cottages, thatched roofs and pretty gardens. The medieval church has an unusual octagonal tower, and the Royal Oak Inn has an interesting collection of horse plough mementoes.

You walk up the main street and then left immediately after the church along Copse Shoot Lane, signposted as a cul-de-sac. At the top end, as the lane swings left to go up to the last bungalow, you keep right to follow an earth pathway going straight on under the trees. This sunken way – for such it is – makes for a pleasant walk, with wild flowers and trees growing up the bank on either side. Where this path bears left you may choose to cut off a corner, thus reducing the length of the walk a little. If so, take the steep path going up to the right. But the sunken way is easier and more attractive.

Barrington Court.

Presently, the path opens out into the fields. Turn right here along the side of a fence, at the end of which you meet a country lane. Those who, earlier, chose the short cut, will emerge at this point too. You now follow the lane to the left (south-west), soon reaching a T-junction. From here the views southwards should not be missed.

There are numerous ways back to Shepton Beauchamp from this point. Those who wish to take the shortest, and miss seeing the village of Stocklinch, should turn left and follow this quiet country lane all the way. Others should follow the track straight on, signposted 'Pound Lane – Public Bridleway'. This route not only leads down another sunken way but also postpones the decision regarding the return journey. Pound Lane leads you down from the T-junction to the village of Stocklinch, bending right then left on its way. After a period of wet weather this bridleway could be a trifle muddy since it is popular amongst horseriders.

Down on the lane that runs through Stocklinch you again have a choice of routes. The easiest way back is left, along the lane away from the village. This takes you uphill, past The

Chantry, a fine stone and thatch cottage on the right. Towards the top of the slope turn left then right and follow the lane all the way back to Shepton.

A longer route, but one that takes in the whole of Stocklinch, is right, along the lane through the village. Follow this all the way round past the little church to the far end, where stands the large church with a tower. From there a footpath leads across the fields to a road where you turn right, and then left along another path to another road. Turn right for Shepton.

A third route employs the footpath that leads from behind The Chantry to the towered church, thence by way of the footpaths already mentioned. But whichever route you choose, make sure you linger awhile in Stocklinch – a village where time seems to have stood still.

Places of interest nearby

Barrington Court is now owned by the National Trust. It is a large Tudor mansion, built by Henry Daubeney who was much inspired by Hampton Court. A gallery runs along the entire length of the attic. After falling into disrepair it was restored, first by Colonel A. Lyle (of Tate and Lyle, the sugar company) who lived here in the 1920s, and then by the National Trust. The interior is now leased as a showroom for a furnishings company. The pretty gardens, re-created with the advice of Gertrude Jekyll, now operate a pick-your-own scheme in summer months.

East Lambrook Manor, just 2 miles to the north-east, has a garden created by the famous plantswoman Margery Fish. It is a lovely 'cottage garden', deservedly listed as Grade I for the purposes of protection. Plants may be purchased from the adjoining nursery.

North of Shepton Beauchamp, just 2 miles distant, is *Westport*. The canal here, built in 1840 to link Hambridge and Westport to the Bristol Channel via the Isle and Parrett rivers, has been carefully restored. The nearby *Hambridge Fishery* has a collection of tropical birds as well as ornamental fish.

Burrow Hill, east of here, near Stembridge, offers fine views across the Somerset Levels.

⑩ **Huish Episcopi**
The Rose and Crown

This pub is known by everyone locally as Eli's and on no account should it be missed. To walk through its main entrance is happily to walk back in time. This is what most pubs would have been like once, and sadly what so few are like today. There is no bar as such. Customers are served from a low central room where bottles and barrels stand over a stone-flagged floor. There is a rabbit warren of rooms, each with old wooden furniture and settles, prints and paintings on the walls and traditional fireplaces. There is a large back room where pool can be played. Children are welcome and are not confined to any particular area.

Eli's is a freehouse, serving a good selection of real ales (including Smiles and Boddingtons) and some of the best Somerset farmhouse cider to be had locally. Country wines are also offered, and the native version of calvados – Somerset cider brandy. The food available is simple but nicely presented and generous in portion, for example, ploughman's lunches, sandwiches, pies and snacks based on toast. Normal pub opening times are kept, except on Fridays and Saturdays when the doors stay open each afternoon as well.

Eileen Pittard (whose father, incidentally, was named Eli) now runs the pub with her children. It has been in her family for over 120 years and across four generations. Both her father and grandfather each held the licence for 55 years, and the atmosphere could not have changed much since their days. The building dates from the early 17th century but it is not known how long it has been a pub. Long may it continue to be one.

Telephone: 0458 250494.

How to get there: Huish Episcopi is joined to the eastern end of the town of Langport. It is 4 miles west of Somerton and 12 miles east of Taunton. The Rose and Crown stands on the A372, at the left-hand side as you leave Langport in the Wincanton direction.

Parking: There is a large pub car park. There is also a free public car park 200 yards away, opposite Huish Episcopi church.

Length of the walk: 2½ miles (or shorter options). OS Landranger map 193 Taunton and Lyme Regis (inn GR 431266).

This route combines a pleasant country stroll along a meandering river bank with an interesting walk through the ancient town of Langport. Just south of Huish Episcopi the river Yeo meets the river Parrett, close to the edge of the Somerton Hills. To the south lie the broad water meadows which form one small part of the Somerset Levels. This is a landscape of deep drainage ditches (called 'rhynes') lined with pollarded willow trees, of peat moors where reed beds flourish, of broad skies and distant hills rising up above the watery plain. This is a positive haven for bird-watchers.

The town of Langport is an old market town and former port, the river Parrett once being navigable to sea-going vessels. There are many historic buildings here, together with the famous 'Hanging Chapel'. For those interested, the town also has its fair share of antique shops and second-hand bookshops.

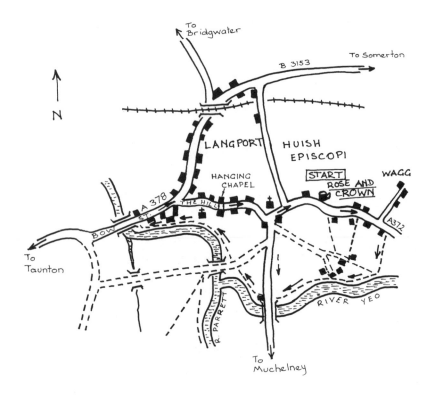

The Walk

From the Rose and Crown there are several routes down to the river Yeo. The easiest is by way of Huish Episcopi church, opposite to which is a lane signposted to Muchelney. Walk down this lane, past the old cottages of the village and a drive to the left leading to a factory warehouse. Then you can either take the next track on the right, which leads directly to Huish Bridge (close to where the rivers Yeo and Parrett meet) or else continue along the lane to a stile on the right (before a Victorian cottage called 'Swanston') and thence along the riverside path signposted to Huish Bridge.

An alternative route begins east of the pub, almost opposite Wagg Drove, a lane coming down from the left. Take the footpath between a stream and Ducks Hill Cottage, through a gate with the sign 'Manor House. Footpath'. Follow this path across the stream, through a gate and thence by fieldsides and stiles to an old sluice. Through the next gate (aiming for Horsey Farm ahead) you soon reach the Yeo river bank. Turn right and follow the path all the way, past the factory warehouses and across the road near 'Swanston'.

There is another route – a footpath meandering through fields, around cottages and between warehouse buildings – but this is not recommended as it is the least attractive of the three.

From the banks of the Yeo there are some pleasant views. The footpath is raised up on top of the levee thus offering clear sightlines over the meadows. To the left is Muchelney church and beyond – on the distant skyline – Windwhistle Hill. To the right is the gloriously decorated tower of Huish Episcopi church. If you have time at the end of the walk have a look inside, where you will see some fine stained-glass windows by the Victorian Pre-Raphaelite Burne-Jones. The name Huish Episcopi, incidentally, is a corruption of the Saxon word 'hiwisc (meaning 'household' or 'homestead) and the Latin word 'episcopus' (meaning 'bishop'). The manorial estate once belonged to the Bishop of Bath and Wells.

The walk westwards of Huish Bridge is along the north bank of the river Parrett (although, initially, you actually follow the side of an overflow channel). Soon the footpath crosses a little stone bridge (over the channel) and proceeds along the ends of a row of back gardens. Be careful not to disturb the anglers along this stretch, for this is a popular place amongst fishermen.

Where the back gardens stop the path opens out across a wide grassy area where a bench seat has been placed, for the use of those who simply want to sit and watch the wildlife go by. Those wishing to cut short the circular walk can turn right here and cross the car park to Langport town centre. Others may like to continue along the river Parrett until, eventually, they meet the main A378 road. At that point will be found a group of converted warehouses and an elegant three-arched bridge. This is the western end of Langport, where once stood the medieval port that gave the town its raison d'être. The name actually meant, in Saxon times, 'long port' or 'long market centre'. The town grew rich on trade in fowl, eels, goose-down and feathers, cider and wool. Even in the Middle Ages the built-up area stretched from here to the church at the top of the hill, ½ mile away.

The Hanging Chapel at Langport.

The return journey to Huish Episcopi is eastwards along Bow Street (the A378) and then up The Hill (straight on at the town centre as the main road bears left). There are many old and interesting buildings along Bow Street and its continuation, Cheapside. In a house next to the National Westminster Bank (once belonging to Stuckey's Bank) was born, in 1826, Walter Bagehot the economist and author of *The English Constitution*. Further along, on the left, is the old market building, space for the stalls being created amongst the columns.

At the top of The Hill is the quiet part of town, dominated by the 15th century church. On the left, at the corner of Priest Lane, is a large old gatehouse building, with a grand clock face set into its upper wall. The old village pump is close by. The views southwards from here, incidentally, should not be missed.

As you continue down the far side of The Hill you walk under the famous Hanging Chapel. This was built in medieval times for a local tradesmen's guild. Later it became a school and is now owned by the Freemasons. And why is it hanging? Well, the archway above which it stands was once the East Gate.

Langport was originally a walled town. The chapel was, in fact, built along the stone ramparts.

There is now an easy downhill walk to Huish Episcopi church and, beyond, to the Rose and Crown. Eli's hospitality is beckoning.

Places of interest nearby

Muchelney Abbey, a little over a mile to the south, is owned by English Heritage and is well worth a visit. Little of the original 8th century abbey church survives, but other parts of this Benedictine monastery can still be seen, including such domestic buildings as the Abbot's lodging and guest house, the kitchen, the latrines building and the south walk of the cloisters. The surrounding village is worth more than a passing glance – note the mullioned windows everywhere – and the nearby Priest's House (National Trust) is a 14th century thatched building which has scarcely altered since it was built.

Two miles south-west of Langport, near Drayton, is *Midelney Manor*. This is a Tudor manor house with a pretty walled garden, a 17th century falcon mews and heronry.

Another 2 miles further away, near Fivehead, is the *West Sedgemoor Reserve*. This is run by the RSPB and consists of a mixture of wet meadowlands and deciduous woodland. There is a hide, a large heronry and a variety of flora, including marsh marigolds and orchids.

For those who enjoy wide and distant horizons there are a couple of good viewpoints nearby, both close to Curry Rivel, 2 miles to the south-west. One is *Red Hill*, owned by the National Trust. The other is the *Burton Pynsent Monument*. This was built in 1765, at the time of William Pitt the Elder. From each place almost the whole of Somerset lies before you.

Roundham
The Traveller's Rest

11

This is a 19th century staging inn built when the present A30 was still the main road from London to Cornwall. It gave a friendly welcome then and continues to do so today. Indeed, outside the pub, along the main road, are various notices and advertising boards designed to entice you in – special menu items, specially low real ale prices, special events or functions. In fact, the whole place is rather special. It is open all day 11 am to 11 pm except on Sundays and Mondays (when more normal pub times are kept), and provides the sorts of refreshments required by every different kind of customer. It is a wonderfully successful mixture of pub, café and good class restaurant. There is one large bar with beams, traditional pub fittings and an open fireplace. Beyond is a skittle alley/function room which acts as a family room, children being very welcome. There is also a pleasant garden behind.

The Traveller's Rest is a freehouse, offering real ales (including Twelve Bore and Bass Special), a wide selection of wines (including carafes of house wine) and draught cider. But it is food that makes the place locally famous. For quality and variety it is unsurpassed. The comprehensive bar menu ranges from soups, snacks, sandwiches and tea-cakes to steaks, roasts and fish dishes, and a full range of sweets. But the specials – listed on the blackboard – are the items to study. There might be a seafood platter, liver and bacon casserole or, for vegetarians, cashew nut casserole with mushrooms. Half-price portions are provided for children. One excellent idea is to offer two-size meals – for curry, chilli or spaghetti bolognaise dishes, for instance, customers can choose between a main portion and a 'snack pot' size. All-day breakfasts are also available. Prices for all the food, and indeed for the beers, are very reasonable.

Telephone: 0460 72580.

How to get there: Roundham is just a hamlet, situated along the A30 main road just 1 mile west of Crewkerne. Chard is 6 miles to the west, Yeovil 9 miles to the north-east. The Traveller's Rest will be found on the left just before you leave Roundham, on the way to Chard.

Parking: There is a large pub car park. Elsewhere in Roundham space is limited for parking, this being a busy main road. However, there is a lay-by on the south side of the A30 to the east of the hamlet.

Length of the walk: 2½ miles. OS Landranger map 193 Taunton and Lyme Regis (inn GR 423098).

The area north of Roundham is extremely pretty, with narrow little valleys and a scatter of mounds and hillocks. The following walk crosses this dissected landscape, winding up, down and between the slopes and across narrow combes along which grow belts of trees. At the far end, the green mound of Castle Hill is circumnavigated, a treeless eminence that would have been a perfect site for an ancient fort.

Apart from two short stretches of road, the route is entirely along bridleways. However, do not expect wide clear tracks. These bridleways are more like footpaths. They cross fields and cut through patches of thicket. After wet weather parts of the route can also be muddy, so strong footwear is recommended.

The Walk

On the other side of the road from the Traveller's Rest, just 100 yards up on the way to Crewkerne, is a gate. This will be found by the first house you reach in that direction. Next to the gate is a signpost, 'Bridleway, Castle Lane 1 mile'. This is the start of your walk, and almost immediately you have fine views straight ahead.

The path runs northwards along the edge of a field, with the hedgerow on your right. This leads down to a rough stile, on the other side of which the path continues down into a valley. This winds slightly as it avoids the grassy slope going up on the left. At the bottom is a gate, leading a way through a thicket that runs across, along the line of a little stream.

The path continues, this time winding uphill, slightly left, towards the skyline. Up to the half-left, on a farther skyline is a grassy knoll. Straight ahead, farther still, is the green dome of Castle Hill. Over to the the right is Fords Croft Farm. All around, the view is very pretty indeed – an undulating landscape in miniature.

Very shortly, the path bears right (at a large round cattle trough) and makes directly for the farm buildings. Upon reaching these you turn left along a firm trackway, keeping the modern barns and cattle sheds – and, soon after, a bungalow too – on your right. The surface underfoot is hard, being a mixture of solid gravel and old tarmac. Follow this trackway all the way to the road. This is a very pleasant stretch. The route dips a little, crosses a narrow, shallow valley where a stream tumbles between the trees, and bears right to run between the bare Castle Hill (on your right) and the wooded Liddon Hill (on your left). Be sure to look behind as you walk along here – there is a lovely view back to the hills beyond Crewkerne.

After reaching the road and turning right (in the direction towards Hinton St George), you are immediately met with yet more views. This time they are left towards Ilminster and ahead towards Merriott, beyond which on the skyline is Ham Hill, complete with its war memorial on top. On clear days you can see the Mendip Hills from here.

The road skirts round the base of Castle Hill and then bears left, to run downhill. About 200 yards down on the right is a gate and signpost marking a bridleway and stating that

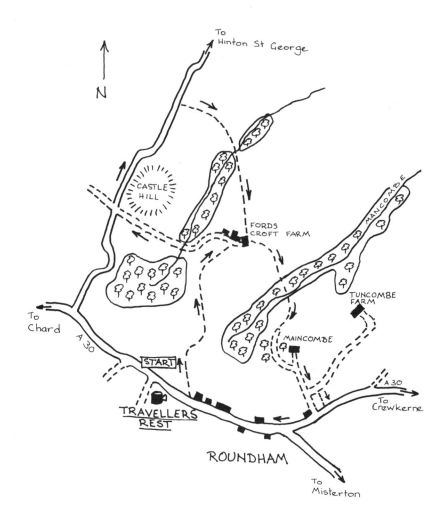

Roundham is 1 mile away. Go through this gate and cross the field. After a very short distance you join a hedge on your left which you follow, in the same direction as before. This path – along the edge of one field – leads on to the next field, through a gate opening. Now aim diagonally across this second field, half-right towards a line of trees.

As you approach these trees a clear way through presents itself in the form of a wide, stony track. This leads down through the thicket, over a little stream, and up the other side,

71

turning as it reaches the next field. Once again, bear half-right and aim diagonally up to the brow of the slope. Soon you will see the barns and sheds of Fords Croft Farm, straight ahead. This is where the route is leading you.

From the farm some people may prefer to turn right and retrace their steps, down the path along which they originally walked, back to Roundham. But this would mean they miss some delightful scenery either side of the wooded valley known as Mancombe.

To complete the circular walk, and to enjoy Mancombe, keep to the left of Fords Croft Farm. Skirt the buildings and continue down into the valley (keeping roughly in the same direction as your route just before reaching the farm). The path – officially a bridleway – is not absolutely clear but you should be able to find the way through the trees and across the stream, using the bridleway signs as a guide.

This is an idyllic little combe, wooded, quiet and totally unspoilt. As you climb up the other side, and rise above the level of the treetops, the view back is lovely – the rolling countryside of south Somerset.

In fact, after you cross Mancombe, and come out of the trees, bear right. This is steep, hummocky terrain, so the route involves some ups and downs, but you should soon see a tractor-rutted trackway dipping down to your right. Follow this round the head of a little side valley and up over a spur, turning slightly to the left as you go. Then you are presented with a choice – continue along the tractor ruts which run down again, along a dip, or else bear left up an alternative route, a gravelly way running up at an angle under some trees. Choose the latter, which is, in fact, the official right of way. The former is a cut-off used by the local farmer.

Follow the gravel track uphill. This veers left to meet a wider pathway, which is, actually, the principle drive to Maincombe House. Turn right. The A30 main road is now immediately ahead. It would be tempting to walk directly there, but the right of way turns left, up the track signposted to Tuncombe Farm, and then almost immediately right along a narrow, earthy path between high hedgerows. At the main road turn right, to return to Roundham. This is a busy road but there is a grass verge most of the way to the Traveller's Rest.

Places of interest nearby

Just 3 miles west of Roundham, along the A30, is *Windwhistle Hill*. From the top are glorious views, down over Somerset to the north, into the Dorset hills to the south. On clear days both the Bristol Channel and English Channel can be seen.

Below Windwhistle is *Cricket St Thomas*. Here, the 18th century manor house is surrounded by informal gardens and a famous wildlife park. Amongst the rare shrubs and trees roam elephants, camels, llamas and, around the lake, wild waterfowl and flamingos. Here also is the National Heavy Horse Centre and a home farm where there are regular demonstrations of old farming techniques and a country life museum. There is a farm shop, a children's adventure playground, a picnic area and café.

Clapton village is 2 miles south of Roundham. The *Clapton Court Gardens* must be among the most beautiful in the West Country, giving year-round colour with rare floral species in a woodland setting. The nearby *Flour Mill* has been in continuous use since 1870. There are guided tours showing the history of milling.

South of Crewkerne is *Higher Folly Farm*, a sheep dairy farm where visitors can see ewes milked and sheeps' milk yoghurt and fudge made.

At Dowlish Wake, 3 miles north-west of Roundham, is found *Perry's Cider Mills* where there is a museum of farm machinery and visitors can watch cider being made. Cider can also be tasted and purchased.

⑫ **Rodney Stoke**
The Rodney Stoke Inn

This large, handsome, Victorian/Edwardian style building is an ideal place to stop and rest, both for motorists and walkers. There is a wide choice of food and drink, the atmosphere is friendly and comfortable, and the opening hours are long. In fact, the Rodney Stoke Inn is open all day, from 11 o'clock onwards, every day. Children are very welcome both inside and out – in the garden are some playthings, like a climbing frame. There is a large snug, or public bar, where locals and 'drinkers only' tend to congregate. Through the glass-panelled doors is a roomy lounge-cum-restaurant where families, those customers eating, and also those having morning coffee or afternoon tea tend to sit. These rooms are dark and plush, with bare stone walls, red cushioned seats and an open fireplace where a real fire can be enjoyed in cold periods. Pictures and brassware are hung up to add to the cosy atmosphere. There are beams but, of course, these are for show rather than for architectural necessity.

The real ales served include Worthington Best and various wines and ciders are offered. Numerous blackboards in the lounge bar, list the food choices, and very tempting they are too. Among the snacks are the ubiquitous ploughman's lunches, together with various salads and 'starter' items like soup, whitebait and garlic mushrooms. The main courses range from the simple (ham, egg and chips, gammon and plaice, for instance) to the more adventurous (like steak and kidney pie, lasagne, quiche and trout). Desserts could include chocolate fudge cake and meringue.
Telephone: 0749 870209.

How to get there: Rodney Stoke lies at the foot of the Mendip Hills between Cheddar (3 miles to the north-west) and Wells (5 miles to the south-east). Glastonbury is 7 miles away to the south. The inn stands on the A371 road, to the right as you approach from Cheddar.

Parking: There is a large pub car park. Vehicles should not be left along the A371 owing to its relative narrowness and amount of traffic. However, motorists may find some spaces down in the lanes towards the church, south of the Rodney Stoke Inn.

Length of the walk: 3 miles. OS Landranger map 182 Weston-super-Mare and Bridgwater (inn GR 484503).

The southern slopes of the Mendip Hills rise fairly steeply from the Somerset Levels to bare, grassy summits. From the tops are superb views across towards Glastonbury, the Brendons, the Quantocks and the Severn Estuary. This area is popular amongst walkers, so the footpaths are well used and well signposted.
This walk climbs the Mendip Edge along a clear, gravel trackway. At the top a little detour takes you to an Iron Age hill fort and settlement, on the slopes of Westbury Beacon. This is one of the highest points on the Mendips. The return follows the West Mendip Way – a well-known long distance footpath – down to the village of Draycott. The last mile is on a track along the edge of the Wedmore meadows. All the ground is firm underfoot. Some stiles need to be crossed, but these should not create any difficulties.

The Walk

The route begins opposite the Rodney Stoke Inn. Take the narrow tarmac lane signposted as a dead-end. It runs straight, with stone wall and hedgerow on either side, and climbs steadily towards the green slopes ahead. Past a couple of buildings on the left, it soon bears left itself, the surface by this time deteriorating to gravel and stone. Further up you will see a vineyard over to the left and the Rodney Stoke Nature Reserve to the right. Continue upwards.

Despite the steep climb this is an easy walk. The trackway is clear and dry and the views behind become increasingly extensive. You may wish to stop frequently to catch your breath. If so, be sure to turn round – the panorama behind and to the left is glorious.

The trackway you are following is an old 'straker way' – a route used in ancient times by local farmers. Cattle and sheep were driven up such ways from the valleys to the hilltops, to enjoy the high pastures when the Levels were too wet. There are many such 'straker ways' in South West England, running up the steep slopes of the moorland ranges – the Quantocks, Brendons and the great masses of Exmoor and Dartmoor. Cattle and sheep are still grazed up on these hills, but the steep south-facing slopes are now also used for growing soft fruit, especially strawberries. The mild climate generally, and the sunny aspect in particular, ensure an early harvest (and therefore a high price) for the crop. Vines, in a few places, are grown for the same meteorological reasons, as well as for the suitably friable soils.

As the track begins to level off you reach a farm gate, marking the end of the stone wall on either side and the end of the 'straker way'. Beyond is the open hillside, still rising gently to the skyline, where a line of trees can be seen along the ridge. Not far away, in front, is a derelict stone building. There is a signpost next to the gate, announcing a footpath going straight on to 'New Road'. You continue straight on as well, although you will not go as far as New Road, which is the lane from Draycott to Priddy.

Walk across the open pasture to the right of the derelict building – once a barn or shepherd's hut. Passing this to your left, you then proceed uphill (bearing slightly left), aiming for the left-hand end of the line of small trees you will see running

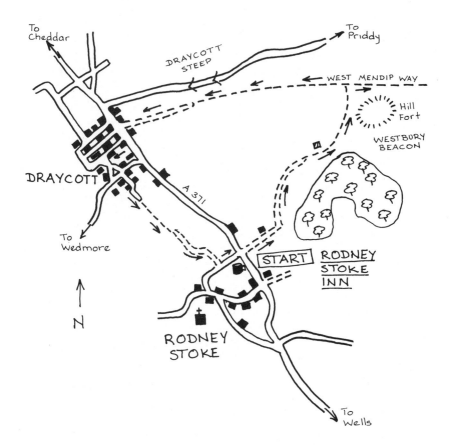

To Cheddar

To Priddy

DRAYCOTT STEEP

WEST MENDIP WAY

Hill Fort

WESTBURY BEACON

DRAYCOTT

A 371

To Wedmore

N

START

RODNEY STOKE INN

RODNEY STOKE

To Wells

along the skyline ahead. These trees, in fact, grow on top of an old stone wall – a boundary hedge for a moorland enclosure.

When you reach the end of this walled tree-hedge you will find a stone stile, and a footpath signpost – Priddy is 2½ miles away. At this point you could turn left and start the downward journey immediately. But after such a climb it would be a pity to miss the summit, Westbury Beacon, especially since it is surmounted by an Iron Age hill settlement. Climb over the stile, therefore, and make your way up (over another stone stile) to the top. You will be richly rewarded.

All around, now, is typical Mendip scenery. The rock underneath is limestone, so the soils are thin and dry, and the grass is short. Northwards you look across a near-treeless plateau towards Cheddar Gorge, eastwards you look across the windswept pastures towards Priddy. The valleys of the Mendips are deeply cut and narrow – you cannot see into them from this flat summit. The Iron Age settlement consists of rough, circular embankment, the ground within being hummocky, with bumps and hollows. The trained eye would probably identify the hut sites. These are likely to have been used in times of strife, when local farmers had to seek the protection of a fortified enclosure.

The journey down begins, of course, with a return to the stone stile at the end of the walled tree-hedge. You will now notice a footpath sign pointing down to Draycott, 1 mile away. The route is very clear, for it follows the long distance footpath called the West Mendip Way. This runs for some 30 miles from Bleadon Hill (Weston-super-Mare) to Wells, using a collection of paths, tracks and country lanes. For much of this distance it follows the line of an ancient trackway.

In Celtic times, and earlier, England's hill ranges were used as trade routes, allowing minerals and agricultural produce to be carried all across Britain, and over to Europe. Tin was brought up from Cornwall and Devon, and here on the Mendips lead and iron ore were mined. Such minerals were transported along tracks, such as the Mendip Way, to the Salisbury Plain and thence by way of the chalk escarpments to the Channel. The famous Pilgrims' Way was, in fact, an ancient route to Dover long before Canterbury became a centre for pilgrimage. Another prehistoric trackway ran along the Cotswolds to the Humber.

All the way down – across several fields and a number of well-marked stone stiles – you aim towards Nyland Hill. You will see this down below and ahead, a rounded, tree-topped knoll rising up from the Levels. To your right, roughly parallel, is a deep little combe, in the bottom of which runs the lane to Priddy. In due course you reach a gate, beyond which the route follows another 'straker way' all the way down to Draycott. The ground underfoot changes from earth to gravel and, eventually, to tarmac. At the bottom, by a war memorial, is the A371 road.

Turn left and then, after about 50 yards, right, down Wet Lane. At the bottom of this, at a junction, turn left, quickly followed by left again, at a fork. This is a little triangle, in fact,

Rodney Stoke church.

where an interesting sunken horse trough will be seen. Cross over the next road and continue down the 'dead-end' road opposite (called Eastville Lane). This takes you through a small housing estate. At the far end the road narrows, continuing in the same direction between some fields.

The route back to Rodney Stoke is now easy, the village church being visible in front. The fields to your right slope gently down to the river Axe, beyond which the meadows stretch to the Wedmore ridge. After a double bend this tarmac-gravel track – for such the road has become – reaches a gate. Beyond is a private garden and house. Worry not. There is a path to the right leading straight on, its entrance being marked by a wooden cross-stile (whose top bar lifts up). At the far end the path widens to a trackway again, grassy at first and then gravelly. In due course it becomes a tarmac lane. Keeping left you will eventually arrive back up on the A371 road. The Rodney Stoke Inn is on your right – it could hardly be nearer.

Places of interest nearby

The area around Rodney Stoke is popular with tourists, so there are many places to visit within a very short distance. *Cheddar* (3 miles north-west) should not be missed, with its gorge, caves, cheese-making demonstrations at its 'Rural Village', its various nature trails and its plethora of gift shops, tearooms and craft centres.

Just 2 miles further on from Cheddar is *Axbridge*, also worth a visit. It has an interesting old market square, many timber-framed buildings and a local museum housed in the 'King John's Hunting Lodge', which is owned by the National Trust.

Beyond Axbridge, at Webbington (8 miles from Rodney Stoke), is the *Wheelwright's Working Museum and Gypsy Folklore Collection*. Close to this, on the A38 road at Lower Weare are the *Ambleside Aviaries and Water Garden* where there is a small lakeside pleasure garden with rare birds, fish, and a pets corner.

To the south-east of Rodney Stoke are the famous *Wookey Hole Caves* where visitors can see, as well as the caves themselves, such attractions as 'fairground memories', a 'magical mirror maze' and an 'old penny arcade'. Above Wookey is *Ebbor Gorge*, with its nature reserve, picnic area and numerous nature trails. Slightly further away is the town of *Wells* with its wonderful cathedral, Bishop's Palace and old streets.

13 Montacute
The Phelips Arms

Named after the Elizabethan family that built nearby Montacute House, this pub is a handsome classical building, situated opposite the main village square. Inside there is a pleasant, comfortable atmosphere. No beams, but there are panelled doors, a timber dado around the large bar room and various pieces of brass and copperware hanging in the fireplace. Daily newspapers hang on a rack for the use of customers. Opposite the main entrance as you go in is the door leading out to the beer garden. Along the courtyard to the right is the family room, which also includes a skittle alley.

The Phelips Arms prides itself on its extensive menu, many of its items being suitable for vegetarians. Additional daily specials, like Thai spiced pork and Torbay plaice, are listed on the blackboard above the mantelpiece. The regular choices are too numerous to itemise fully, but include garlic mushrooms, devilled prawns and Chinese spring rolls amongst the starters; lasagne, 'boozy beef' pie, ham steak with mustard butter, and

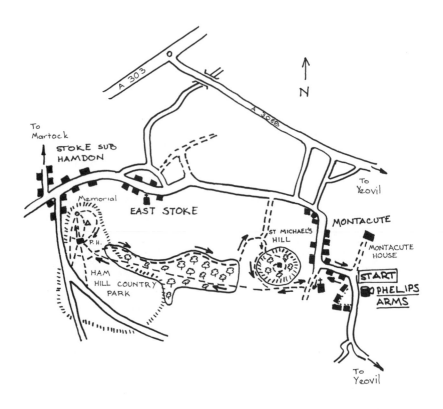

roast chicken amongst the 'Old Faithfuls'; Jamaican banana custard, treacle tart and rice pudding amongst the sweets. Apart from the standard snacks, like ploughman's lunches and various kinds of sandwiches, there is also a mouth-watering list of foreign dishes. The pub, which keeps normal opening times, belongs to the Dorset brewery of Palmers and hence serves an excellent range of real ales including Bridport and Tally Ho! Draught cider is also served.

Telephone: 0935 822557.

How to get there: Montacute will be found just a couple of miles from the western outskirts of Yeovil, close to the main A303 trunk road. It is most easily approached from the A3088, using the turning south of Tintinhull. To reach Montacute from the Ilminster direction, one must first drive through Stoke sub

Hamdon. The Phelips Arms is located east of the church, near the entrance to Montacute House.

Parking: There is no pub car park but the village square (more like a triangle) which is opposite the main entrance is gravelled and given over entirely to car parking. Other parking spaces can be found elsewhere in the village.

Length of the walk: 2½ miles (or longer options). OS Landranger map 193 Taunton and Lyme Regis (inn GR 498168).

This is a lovely walk, to be enjoyed any time of year. There are fine views to be had across the Somerset countryside. On clear days the Quantocks and Mendip Hills can be seen over the Levels and, to the north-east, King Alfred's Tower on the Wiltshire border. All the footpaths used are clear and well signposted but cross undulating ground, with some fairly steep slopes.

The walk is to Ham Hill Country Park and back, by way of a very pleasant stretch of hillside woodland. Those who do not wish to undertake the entire circuit, and those with prams or wheelchairs, may care to park their cars at Ham Hill itself and simply enjoy the stroll around the hilltop and the panoramic views.

The Walk

Walk through the village and take the 'No Through Road' that runs between the church and the King's Arms pub. A little way up this lane you will come to a footpath signpost, pointing both straight on (continuing up the track) and right (through a gate and past the front of Abbey Farm). Follow the latter and go through the gate, notwithstanding the 'Private Road' sign attached to it. You should note that the signpost indicates a path to Hedgecock Hill Wood – for this is, indeed, the direction you want.

The Abbey Farmhouse is of ancient foundation – built by the monks of the nearby Clunaic priory which, itself, was established by the Norman baron, the Count of Mortaign, in the early Middle Ages. This farmhouse, and some monastic ruins near Montacute House, are all that survived Henry VIII's Dissolution of the Monasteries. Beyond Abbey Farmhouse another gate takes you through to a clear track leading uphill to a grassy field. Continue across this field, keeping the wooded hill up to your right and an attractive little valley down to your left. The wooded hill is, in fact, St Michael's Hill which you will see more clearly at the end of your walk.

Aim for the next wooded hill in front where, at its left-hand edge, you will find a stile (taking care to appreciate the view to your right on the way). Beyond this stile the route becomes very easy to find and extremely pretty to follow. A clear footpath winds uphill through the trees, marked intermittently by yellow arrow discs. Over two more stiles (the second taking the path through a wire fence), you climb steadily with occasional glimpses to the right, through the trees, of the view over the Somerset Levels.

These are the Hedgecock Hill Woods. A medieval hedge once ran along the length of this woodland, dividing the parishes of Stoke and Montacute. Little now remains of that hedge, but the woods are lovely to behold, especially in spring when the undergrowth blossoms and in autumn when the leaves turn golden.

Past an old metal pulley post (a remnant of the days of quarrying) the path levels off, going up and down over the humps in the forest floor. In due course you reach an old stone wall, much overgrown. Follow this up, the path running along its left-hand side. At the top the route opens out into an area of grassy humps and hollows, a confusing landscape of hillocks and dips. These are the old quarry workings of Ham Hill Country Park.

These 150 acres of woodland and grassland are managed by South Somerset District Council and contain car parks, toilets (with disabled facilities), picnic sites, a barbecue area and even a public house (the Prince of Wales). Rising to 300 ft above sea level the L-shaped hilltop boasts the largest Iron Age fort in Britain, the ramparts stretching for 3 miles. The Romans built a villa here (the hill overlooks the Foss Way) and, during the Middle Ages, a village grew up (called South Ameldon), becoming famous as the venue of an annual fair. Sadly, little remains of all this early activity, 2,000 years of quarrying having obliterated much of the archaeological evidence.

There are numerous paths around the old ramparts and quarry hummocks and you are free to walk at will. The view from the monument (a war memorial), which stands at the

Abbey Farm, Montacute.

northern end, overlooking Stoke sub Hamdon, is well worth the extra ½ mile added to your circular walk.

The journey back is by way of a footpath which runs along the bottom edge of Hedgecock Hill Wood, just within the line of trees. To reach this you can start at the Prince of Wales, outside which is an interesting panorama board, naming the features in the view below.

Following the footpath signpost to Montacute, you descend by way of a narrow track through the undergrowth. Bearing left you soon reach the overgrown stone wall you accompanied on your way up. Now you accompany it again on your way down. But, at the point where this wall ends, do not continue in the same direction. Instead, walk steeply downhill. At the bottom of the slope you meet the wide footpath mentioned earlier – the one that runs along the edge of the wood. Follow this for some way, keeping the open fields to your left, beyond which are views across the river Yeo towards the Somerton Hills.

The footpath winds its way past a derelict pumping station, eventually reaching the eastern edge of the woodland. There it turns sharply left, down to meet a gravel track, reached through a metal kissing-gate. Turn right along this track but, shortly (where it bends left to descend to the tarmac road) right again, climbing a short flight of steps to a gate. St Michael's Hill is now in front, a wooded mound reached across a grassy field.

The way back to Montacute village is round the base of St Michael's Hill (keeping its trees to your left) to the far side, where you will find the track you took at the beginning of the walk, running down to Abbey Farmhouse. But if you have time, and the inclination, do make the effort to climb this remarkable eminence. A gate leads to a gravel track which climbs through the rising woodland.

Now owned by the National Trust, the hill was a Saxon holy place, where Tofig, King Cnut's standard bearer, discovered a flint crucifix. That was later carried to Waltham Abbey in Essex, where it became the focal point for pilgrimages. The tower that now surmounts St Michael's Hill is no remnant of the Norman castle that once stood on top, but a folly built in 1760. The Greek inscription above the door means 'look out' and, by climbing the spiral staircase inside, you certainly gain a wonderful view over the treetops. Incidentally, the Normans called this hill 'Mons Acutus' (meaning 'pointed hill') from which we get our present village name 'Montacute'.

Places of interest nearby

Montacute House itself really should not be missed. Now owned by the National Trust it is a glorious example of Elizabethan architecture. It contains 16th and 17th century paintings, furniture and tapestries, a display on the top floor of paintings loaned by the National Portrait Gallery, and a Long Gallery which, at 189 ft, is said to be the longest in England. The formal gardens are very pleasant and the tearooms homely.

A little over a mile to the north is another National Trust property: *Tintinhull House* is not open to the public but its garden is. This is a delight throughout the year, its formal layout complemented by a pool, loggia and yew hedges.

At *Stoke sub Hamdon* (2 miles to the west) the National Trust also owns the 14th century priory, where the Great Hall, part of the chantry house and a thatched barn all survive.

South of Ham Hill, close to Westbury Farm, is the site of a deserted village called *Witcombe*. Destroyed by the Black Death, its hummocks are of great interest to archaeologists.

Glastonbury
The Mitre Inn

The search for this pub – down a Glastonbury side street – is well worth the trouble. It is a friendly, comfortable place where children are welcome, the food is excellent and the prices reasonable. Recently refurbished, the Mitre Inn has a modern yet traditional feel. The tables in the bar are all made fom the frames of old treadle sewing machines, and the chairs are wooden with cushioned seats. There is one main bar in the front, behind which is a further room. Around the other side of the bar a corridor leads through to a 'snug' bar and skittle alley. Families use these back rooms, which are pleasantly quiet.

Belonging to the Usher's Brewery, this pub keeps normal opening times. The real ales served include John Smith's and Ushers own Founders. The draught cider is Inch's Stonehouse, and various wines are also available. But the tour de force is the Mitre Inn's extensive and delicious food provision. Regular menus are set out on the tables and daily specials are written up on the blackboard. And what a choice! Apart from the 'usuals', like ploughman's lunches, soups, jacket potatoes and so forth, there are hotpots, lasagne, steaks and various fish dishes. Starters might include garlic mushrooms and fried potato skins with dips, desserts could be banana and toffee pie or 'meringue surprise'. This being Glastonbury, numerous vegetarian meals are also served, like cheese and onion casserole or cheese and broccoli quiche. Children's meals and portions are available, too.

Telephone: 0458 831203.

How to get there: Glastonbury is not hard to find – you can see the Tor for miles around. It is 5 miles south-west of Wells and 8 miles from Shepton Mallet. Yeovil is 15 miles away to the south, Bridgwater 12 miles away to the west. The Mitre Inn stands in Benedict Street (west of the town centre), next to the church.

Parking: There is a small pub car park. There are also numerous public, meter car parks around the town. Further from the shops, beyond the yellow lines, vehicles can be parked freely along the residential streets.

Length of the walk: 2½ miles (or longer options). OS Landranger map 182 Weston-super-Mare and Bridgwater (inn GR 498388).

With its heady mixture of monastic history, biblical associations, Arthurian legend, mystic folklore and earth-force mythology, Glastonbury really should not be missed. The town itself has the abbey ruins, numerous medieval buildings and a rural life museum. Beyond are the Tor, surmounted by the ruins of St Michael's chapel, Chalice Well, said to be the hiding place of the Holy Grail, and the Holy Thorn, thought to have been planted, originally, by Joseph of Arimathaea.

This walk can be divided into two parts. The outward journey is the ascent and descent of Wearyall Hill, upon which will be found the Holy Thorn. The return journey is a level stroll along the river Brue. Thus, there are wide views to be had, and gentle meadow scenery with water wildlife. Throughout the route the paths are clear and firm underfoot.

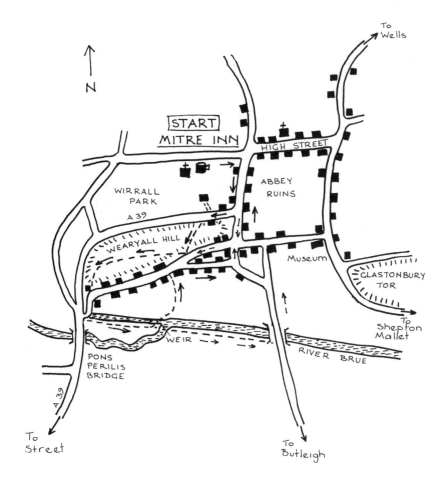

The Walk

Outside the Mitre Inn turn right up Benedict Street and then right again along Magdalene Street. The remains of the old Benedictine abbey will be seen over to the left. Though founded in the depths of the Dark Ages, when Christianity first spread across Saxon England, most of the ruins seen today are Norman in origin. The best preserved building is the Abbot's Kitchen, which dates from the 14th century. Legend says that King Arthur was buried in the abbey precincts, a plaque now marking the spot. Historians have cast doubt on the claim, by the monks of the 12th century, that they had found the tomb of the monarch and his Queen, Guinevere. The discovery too conveniently helped the abbey's fortunes!

At the end of Magdalene Street, where the main road turns sharply right to become Street Road (the road to Street), you have a choice. You can either walk along this main road until you reach the bottom of Wearyall Hill on the left, just after passing the superstore on the right, or you can walk up the residential road ahead (Fishers Hill), turning up the first road you reach on the right (Hill Head). The first option involves a very steep climb up a grassy slope to a stile at the beginning of the ridge path. The second option means a much more gradual ascent, on pavement, to the same stile, over which you climb.

From the stile to the top of Wearyall Hill is a superb, exhilarating walk along the ridge. Extensive views on either side, and a good view back, across to Glastonbury Tor, cause you to stop, frequently, and marvel. Down below to the left is the river Brue, along the side of which you will shortly be making your return to the Mitre Inn. Beyond and above this is the Samuel Hood Monument near Compton Dundon. On the skyline ahead are the Brendon Hills and Quantocks, to the right are Brent Knoll, Wales (if you are lucky with the visibility) and, further round, the Mendips. Towards the top of Wearyall Hill are some bench seats, so you can rest whilst enjoying the far horizons.

Wearyall Hill – or Wirral Hill as it is also known – is said to be the landing place of Joseph of Arimathaea. In those days of course, and until medieval times, the Levels were under water and sea-going vessels could sail this far into Somerset. The story goes that, after a long voyage, Joseph's boat dropped anchor by these slopes, the tired crew being 'weary all', and in need of rest. The stave that Joseph subsequently thrust into the grass later took root and blossomed. The Holy Thorn which you now pass, on your way up to the top of the hill, is a descendant of that original plant, the earlier one having been cut down by Cromwell's Puritans.

The descent is easy. Continue over the top of Wearyall and down the ridge on the other side. A clear footpath over the grass leads directly to a stile (to the right of a little group of trees) and then beyond, to run down behind some large houses on your left. In the bottom corner, past those houses, a short flight of

The Abbots Kitchen, Glastonbury Abbey.

steps leads down to the road. This is the bottom of Roman Way. Turn right towards the busy main road.

Fortunately, you do not actually reach that main road. As the end of Roman Way bends to meet the A39, at the point where it crosses over the river Brue (Pomparles Bridge, otherwise known as Pons Perilis Bridge) you will see a stile down to your left. This leads to a clear path that runs along beside a narrow channel, which is in fact a mill stream. You now have a very pleasant walk across the river meadows to Clyce Hole Weir. Some people might prefer, instead, to ignore the stile and continue to the gate, immediately before the bridge. This leads through to a path which follows the north bank of the river Brue itself, on the top of the raised levee. This route is just as pleasant but might lead you into disturbing the local angling fraternity. The Brue is a popular fishing waterway.

At Clyce Hole Weir you can decide whether or not to lengthen the circular walk. To keep the total distance to the estimated 2½ miles, turn left, and go over the stile. Should you wish to add another mile to your walk, continue along the Brue, this time keeping the river to your left – that is, along the south bank. This extra section will take you directly to the Butleigh road, where you can turn left back to Glastonbury.

From the stile the 'proper' circular walk continues along a footpath which bends to the right, over a stone/concrete bridge and then proceeds diagonally across a field (keeping Glastonbury Tor half-right in the distance). In the far corner a stile leads the path left, over a second stile and then up a grassy field towards the houses. There a third stile takes you up a gravel path to the road. Turn right, along a residential road, to a fork.

From here the easy way back to Glastonbury town centre is to go straight on (along Tor View Avenue) and then turn left at the end (down Fishers Hill to Magdalene Street). The more adventurous, however, may prefer to bear left at the fork, up Hill Head. This will take you up to the beginning of the ridge path that leads up Wearyall. Cross the stile here and walk down the steep grassy slope to the superstore in Street Road, where you turn right.

Places of interest nearby

The adjacent town of *Street* is the home of Clarks shoes. In part of the old factory there is now a shoe museum and many of the shops in the High Street sell bargain 'seconds' direct from the manufacturers. A little to the south of Street is *Ivythorne Hill*, owned by the National Trust. There are pleasant views from here. Neighbouring *Walton Hill* has a windmill.

At *Meare*, 3 miles north-west of Glastonbury, is the Abbot's Fish House – a medieval building once owned by the monks of Glastonbury Abbey. Meare was at one time situated on an island in the marshes, and two separate sites have been discovered of prehistoric lake villages. Also to be found here is the Sweet Track – the remnants of a causeway 6,000 years old. This was made out of logs and represents the earliest man-made road so far found in Western Europe.

Just 5 miles north of Glastonbury is the old town of *Wells*, famous for its abbey and the Bishop's Palace. Close by is *Wookey Hole* where there are nature trails, a museum and, of course, the limestone caves.

15 Charlton Adam
The Fox and Hounds

A very friendly and pleasant pub this, popular with both villagers and travellers passing through. Between the large car park and main entrance is a beer garden with tables and chairs, and a children's play area with slide, swings and climbing frame. Inside all is wood – beams, furniture, bar – very cosy when the open fires are ablaze. There is one main bar room but also a large family room where the pool table stands. To one side of the building there is a skittle alley and function room.

The Fox and Hounds is a freehouse serving real ales, like Boddingtons and Marston's Pedigree, draught cider and a small selection of country wines. The food offered is excellent, both in variety and quality. Apart from the regular menu, which includes ploughman's lunches, soups, pizzas, lasagne, jumbo sausages, jacket potatoes and various types of sandwiches, there are daily 'specials' written up on the blackboard. Breaded pork with Stilton might be available, or perhaps barbecued pork spare ribs. But whatever you choose, it is liable to be wholesome, healthy and home-made.

Normal pub opening times are observed. Food is always available and a welcoming atmosphere ever present. Children's menus are offered and one day a week there is a senior citizens' special three-course lunch, very reasonably priced.

Telephone: 0458 223466.

How to get there: Charlton Adam stands just 3 miles east of Somerton and 8 miles north of Yeovil. The main A37 road passes close by, and the A303 trunk road is 2 miles to the south. The Fox and Hounds is situated at the eastern end of the village, on the left as you approach from the A37.

Parking: The pub car park has space for about 30 cars. Vehicles can also be left at the roadside anywhere in the village, provided no obstruction is created.

Length of the walk: 3 miles (or shorter options). OS Landranger map 183 Yeovil and Frome (inn GR 542288).

This walk circumnavigates the two villages of Charlton Adam and Charlton Mackrell, using clear footpaths across fields and country lanes. There are just a few stiles to be negotiated, and the ground underfoot is generally firm. Those wishing to take a shorter walk (and those pushing wheelchairs or prams), may like simply to stroll amongst the lanes of the two villages, where there is plenty of interest to see.

Charlton Adam and Charlton Mackrell are situated on the eastern end of the Somerton Hills. They have a number of attractive, old buildings, including farms and horse stables, and two handsome churches. All around is pretty scenery, with views across unspoilt countryside.

The Walk

A gate, stile and footpath signpost, opposite the back door to the Fox and Hounds, mark the beginning of the footpath. But take care to follow the path that goes straight on (bearing slightly left along the edge of the field) and not the one (less distinct) that goes off to the right, diagonally across the middle of the field. Keeping the back gardens, the thicket and a small stream immediately to your left, you will soon reach a stile in the corner of the field. Cross this and continue in the same

94

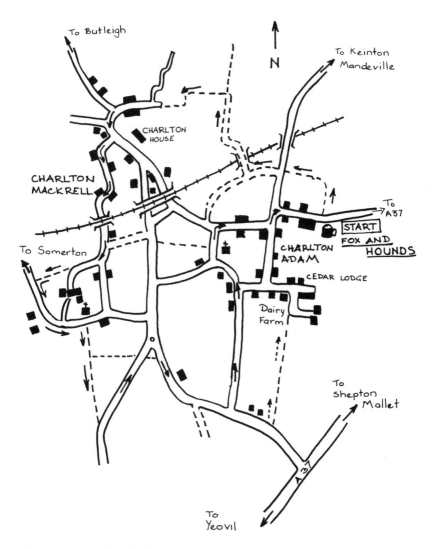

direction (gradually bearing left) with the trees to your left and the field to your right. Where the trees end you will find another stile. On the far side the footpath continues across the edge of the next field to a farm gate. Beyond this is the road.

Across the road, almost opposite, you will see a clear track, firm and gravelly. Take this, as it bends left to run alongside the railway line and then sharply right to cross a bridge over that same railway line. This, incidentally, is the main Inter-city line from London to Taunton. Continue along the gravel track, noting how it bends first to the left then to the right. It is, in fact, running between fields, half hidden by the hedge on either side.

Ignoring the tractor ruts, which cross your route on their way to a quarry yard on the right, you will soon come to the end of the gravel track. Fear not. There is a stile on the left. Beyond this a footpath leads along two sides of a field (hedge on your right) eventually meeting a tractor-made trackway (the same one that you crossed over a moment ago). This leads to a tarmac road, close to a bungalow. Continue down this residential road, past some small industrial buildings on the right, to reach a main junction.

This is Charlton Mackrell. The village is a pleasant, quiet place with a mixture of old and new buildings, some thatched cottages and a historic hostelry (now the Greyhound Inn). At the centre is the handsome, classical-style Charlton House, surrounded by its pretty gardens.

Turning left at the road junction, you will now walk around the perimeter wall of Charlton House. Opposite the front of the building, choose the lane that passes the village stores. This bends left by an old red telephone box and the village hall and passes a number of modern houses. A further right bend leads you down to the edge of the village and round the corner to take you under the railway line.

About 100 yards beyond the railway bridge a clear track leads off to the left, beside a farm. At this point you have a choice. If you wish to cut the walk short, turn up this track. After a while this will bring you to a road across which (almost opposite) a footpath will take you over a field back to Charlton Adam church. If, on the other hand, you wish to continue the circular walk as planned, ignore this track and proceed up the lane that shortly leads off to the right. A wooden post at the corner names this lane as Wellham Road, and it leads up between two stone pillars. There is a pleasant view of Charlton Mackrell church on the left.

At the point where Wellham Road bends left, to head towards some farm buildings (actually, the back of Charlton Mackrell Court), go straight on along a narrow footpath which runs

Lytes Cary Manor.

between an old iron fence on the right and a yew tree and thicket on the left. Now, keeping the fence to your right, continue in a fairly direct route, through a kissing-gate, across the edge of a field, through another kissing-gate and onto the tarmac road. Turn left and walk up to the church. Turn right (south) along a bridleway signposted to Lytes Cary. This is a clear, straight track that leads down, and then up, across a valley and on to meet the tarmac road. A footpath leading off to the left, at the bottom of the valley, has faded into the landscape. This could be taken but is not recommended.

At the tarmac road turn left, back towards Charlton Adam, and then – at the edge of the village, where a mini-roundabout accommodates a road fork – right. A short stretch of trackway could be used to cut the corner, but this might be muddy. The lane climbs up a hill, past a row of thatched cottages on the left, and then levels off to reveal views all around.

There are now two routes back to the Fox and Hounds. Those wishing to keep to footpaths can continue down the lane eastwards and then, beyond the houses, turn left through a gate along a path signposted to Cedar Lodge. This route leads down the edge of a field, eventually coming out at Breach Dairy Farm, where you can turn left down a gravel lane to the village. Those wishing to take a closer look at Charlton Adam itself, can turn left (north) past Fields End Boarding Kennels. This lane leads directly to the village. The former route gives views eastwards towards Cadbury Castle, the latter route gives views westwards to Charlton Mackrell.

These two Charlton villages have ancient foundations. In Saxon times they were tuns (farmsteads) owned by ceorls (free peasants) – hence the name 'Ceorltun' originally – and in the Middle Ages they were manorial estates owned by Normans, the Fitz Adam family and the Mackerel family. Both have some ancient buildings – medieval farms, old manor houses (like the one known as The Abbey) and yeomen's cottages. Even the Fox and Hounds itself dates back to the 16th century, part of it being an old cider house.

Places of interest nearby

Lytes Cary Manor, just a mile to the south, was the home of Sir Henry Lyte, author of the *New Herbal,* the most important horticultural book of Tudor times. Only a part of the original mansion survives, including the Great Hall and Chapel. The attractive gardens were laid out in the early 20th century following an Elizabethan style. The property is owned by the National Trust.

The *Dundon Beacon Nature Reserve,* near Butleigh, 3 miles to the north-west, is run by the Somerset Trust for Nature Conservation. Permits are required for entry but a visit is well worth while. There are ancient woodlands, areas of open down-land flora and good views over Sedgemoor to Glastonbury Tor.

Three miles to the south, close to the Podimore Visitors Centre on the A303, is Yeovilton. Here is the famous *Fleet Air Arm Museum* and RNAS airfield. Old weapons, uniforms and historic aircraft are on show, together with Concorde 002.

Those interested in archaeology may like to visit *East Lydford,* 2 miles away to the north-east. Here, close to the Roman Foss Way, are the remains of a medieval church and a good example of ridge and furrow, evidence of the feudal farming system.

Evercreech Junction
The Natterjack Inn

This was once called The Railway Hotel – back in the days when Evercreech Junction was actually a railway junction. The old Somerset and Dorset line ran through here, and connected up with the Midland Railway line coming down from Bath. When those lines were closed in the 1960s this pub became The Silent Whistle. The present name dates from the 1970s, when the whole place was refurbished. Today it is a very friendly, comfortable establishment with an excellent reputation for its food.

The interior decor is not Victorian, as might have been expected with such a building, but modern traditional. There are bare stone walls, with high-level book shelves, beams in the ceiling, with a wheel set into the plaster, wooden furniture and a log-burning stove. Guns and old prints adorn the walls. There is one large bar room at the front. Beyond – where families prefer to sit – is a 'No Smoking' area and restaurant, reached down a couple of steps. Children are very welcome and the

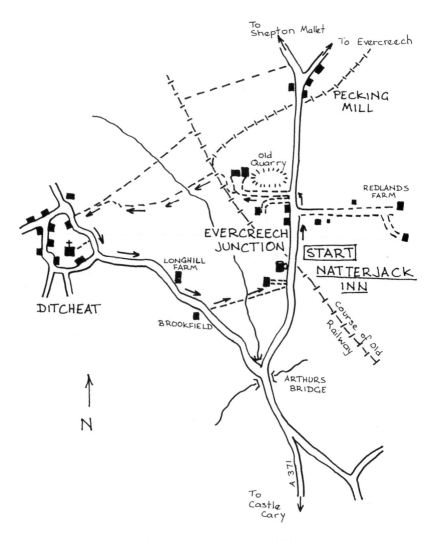

garden contains a climbing frame and slide.

The Natterjack Inn is a freehouse, where normal pub opening times are kept. Real ales (Butcombe and London Pride) and draught ciders are served, and a range of liqueur coffees. But it is the food on offer that makes this place special. There is a wide choice, and everything is freshly cooked and well presented. The regular menu consists of a 5-page book, listing all kinds of snacks and main courses, ploughman's lunches, sandwiches, jacket potatoes, pies, steaks, quiches, curries, fish dishes and so on. A full children's menu is also listed. In addition, daily selections are displayed on a blackboard: fisherman's pie, chicken with cheese and mushroom sauce, mixed grill and suchlike. There is a display case full of desserts and extras might include sticky toffee meringue. Delicious!

Telephone: 0749 860253.

How to get there: Evercreech Junction is situated on the A371 just 1½ miles south of Evercreech. Shepton Mallet is 5 miles to the north, Glastonbury 9 miles to the west. The Natterjack Inn stands on the western side of the main road, on the right as you approach from Shepton Mallet.

Parking: There is a large pub car park. Vehicles should not be left elsewhere along the main road, owing to the volume of traffic. There are, however, numerous lay-bys close to the old railway station.

Length of the walk: 2½ miles. OS Landranger map 183 Yeovil and Frome (inn GR 639365).

The route of this gentle stroll is westwards to the village of Ditcheat, where there are a host of old and attractive cottages, an interesting church dating back to Norman times, and a manor house of great medieval charm. Apart from a short stretch of country lane the route follows footpaths across farmland. This necessarily involves some stile climbing. Most of these footpaths are well marked. Throughout, there are pleasant views all round, for hills rise up in all directions.

The Walk
Immediately to the north of the Natterjack Inn is the old railway station of Evercreech Junction (now converted to domestic use) and sundry other buildings connected with the great age of steam. Those interested in old railways, industrial archaeology, or just nostalgia, should linger awhile and look round. The original name board for the station can still be seen, as can the Victorian junction 'sheds', and the alignment of the old track, now overgrown.

The Somerset and Dorset line opened in 1863 to link Burnham-on-Sea to Poole, with the purpose of connecting passengers from Wales (using a ferry from Cardiff) to France (using another ferry to Cherbourg). This traffic, however, never really materialised and so the line was not a great success. In 1874 a link line was built from Evercreech to Bath (run by the Midland Railway Company) and it was from this date that the hamlet of Evercreech Junction grew up.

The beginning of the walk runs through the heart of the old Evercreech Junction sidings. Continuing northwards along the A371, you pass, over to the left, all the industrial buildings and yards that once serviced the trains. Passing the track to Redlands Farm over to the right, you come to a couple of these cottages on the left – the Laurels and Hillward. Immediately after these, turn left down a tarmac drive that runs to a small industrial site. Do not take the gravel track that runs alongside Hillward. A little way down is a pair of high metal gates, nearly always kept open. If, for any reason, they should be closed and locked, climb over the short fence on the left, using it as a stile.

Continue along this tarmac drive as it swings right to enter a fenced-off commercial compound, through some more metal gates. This time you do not go through. Instead, follow the very clear footpath that leads off at an angle to your left. This runs along the outside of the perimeter fence and then dips left to a metal farm gate. At this point you are standing on the old course of the S and D line. Immediately to your right was the place where the Bath line joined the S and D – faint traces of the alignment can be made out in the grass and along by the hedge.

You now go through the gate and continue in almost a straight line towards Ditcheat. For most of the way you follow the edges of fields, climbing stiles as you go from one field to another. The route is fairly clear throughout.

Along the edge of the first field you follow the hedge on your left. In the second field, after crossing two stiles and a bridge over a small stream, you continue in the same direction, meeting another hedge which you then follow to your right. Along this stretch, as you rise over the brow of a slight hill, Ditcheat church can be seen ahead, its tower almost hidden amongst the trees. Another pair of stiles and a plank bridge (with metal rail) lead through to the third field – a small one which

Part of Ditcheat village.

you cross diagonally half-right to a further stile.

The right of way across the fourth field goes diagonally to a distant stile, half-right, close to the corner. However, you may find this field ploughed and sown. If so, keep to the edge by turning right then, in due course, left. You may find the arrow markers direct you this way in any case, to join another footpath coming down from the right.

Across the last two fields you stay at the edge, all the time keeping the hedge to your left. Another plank bridge and stile divide these two fields but the route is very clear. When you meet the road you will find that you are at the northern end of Ditcheat. To see the village and visit the church, turn right and then, at the junction, left. To miss the village and continue directly with the circular walk, turn left and then, at the next junction, left again.

You now come to the only part of the walk involving tarmac – this quiet stretch along the lane that leaves Ditcheat in an easterly direction. It is not a long stretch, however, and the lane is not busy. In fact, it is very pleasant, with views all round and Creech Hill ahead, on the skyline.

Continue down this lane past Longhill Farm, on the left, until you reach a point where it swings to the right. There is a bungalow called Brookfield on this bend. Opposite this building is a gateway (on the left, at the outside of the bend). Your footpath back to the Natterjack Inn leads off from this point and, in fact, you can just see the roof of the pub in the distance, between the trees.

Cross the field at an angle, keeping the Natterjack to your half-left. Down in the bottom you will find a pathway leading through the hedgerow and an old plank bridge across a stream. On the far side follow the field edge up, skirting a little orchard to your left. At the end of the hedge (where it turns sharply left) a field stretches ahead and the A371 road is no distance away. The right of way crosses at an angle (half-left) to a point where the farm track, over to your left, meets the main road. From there the Natterjack car park is now just a few yards away.

Places of interest nearby

Immediately north of Evercreech Junction, at Southwood, is *Cutterne Mill*. This is a privately owned watermill, built in 1628. The machinery, however, dates from Victorian times. There is a folk museum here, showing the mill's history, together with displays of old costumes and photographs. Outside is a pets corner, a nature trail, a picnic area and a shop selling local crafts.

At Cranmore (5 miles to the north), east of Shepton Mallet, is the well-known *East Somerset Railway*, founded by the wildlife artist David Shepherd. Visitors can see the old railway station and workshops, numerous steam locomotives displayed in the engine sheds, and a special 'African Experience' which includes some famous trains from southern Africa. In summer months steam trains are run down the line to Mendip Vale. There is also an exhibition of wildlife prints by David Shepherd in the old signal box. A children's play area, picnic site, gift shop and restaurant are also provided.

Pilton Manor Vineyard (4 miles north-west of Evercreech Junction) was planted in 1966 on a site first used for vines by Glastonbury Abbey in 1189. Today there are wine tastings, lectures, guided tours, and an exhibition of wine-making. A positive must!

17 Castle Cary
The Horse Pond Inn

This is a traditional town pub. It is not olde worlde and it is not rustically chintzy. It is dark and comfortable, plainly furnished and warmly decorated. It has something of an Edwardian feel about it – perhaps because of the patterned glass in the room dividers. The public bar, with a door at the front, and the lounge bar, with a door down the side, are in fact interconnected in open-plan fashion. At the back, down some steps, is another room used as a dining area. Children are allowed in this back room, and in the games room beyond.

The Horse Pond Inn, which is a freehouse, keeps slightly longer than normal pub opening times, 10.30 am – 3 pm and 5.30 pm – 11 pm. Morning coffee is served. The real ales on offer include Marston's Pedigree, John Smith's and Old Speckled Hen. Cider is also on draught. Extensive normal menus – for bar snacks and restaurant meals – are thoughtfully displayed outside, next to the public bar door. Inside, daily 'specials' are also written up on a blackboard. And what a choice you are given! Amongst the 'quick bites' are rolls, sandwiches, things on toast and jacket potatoes. Amongst the regular meals are omelettes, steaks, scampi, chicken Kiev, and 'specials' might include a curry or hotpot. Vegetarians are catered for, with items like wheat and walnut casserole, and children's menus are offered. Traditional roast beef is always cooked on Sundays and Wednesdays. All these meals are home-made, freshly cooked and well presented. Prices are reasonable, too.

Telephone: 0963 350318.

How to get there: Castle Cary is 5 miles north-west of Wincanton and 7 miles south of Shepton Mallet. Yeovil is 12 miles to the south-west. The town stands close to, but not on, the A371, which runs a little to the east of its town centre. The Horse Pond Inn stands at the centre of town, opposite – would you believe – the horse pond.

Parking: There is a small car park behind the pub, reached by way of a side alley. There is also a large public car park just 100 yards away to the south (away from the town centre).

Length of the walk: 2 miles. OS Landranger map 183 Yeovil and Frome (inn GR 640322).

Immediately to the south of Castle Cary, and overlooking the town, is the long hump of Lodge Hill. This walk goes up, along and down this hill, giving superb views all around, towards the Mendips and Glastonbury, to Wiltshire and King Alfred's Tower, to Dorset, Windwhistle Hill and the Blackdowns. The climb is by way of a clear, gravel farm track, which skirts around the southern end of the hill, rising gradually all the time. The descent is along a footpath which goes steeply down a grassy slope. Some people may wish to return the same way as the ascent, others may prefer the steep path both up and down. There are bench seats along the summit, where you can sit and admire the view. The walk would be especially exhilarating on a warm summer evening when a good sunset is in prospect.

Castle Cary itself is an interesting little town and repays a tour round.

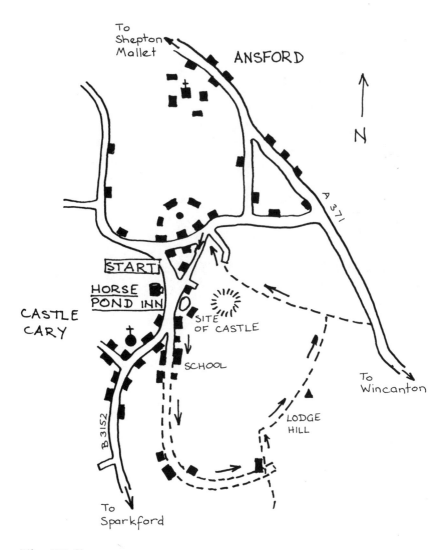

The Walk

Turn right outside the Horse Pond Inn and walk south along the B3152 main road, away from the town centre. Opposite All Saints church, whose spire dominates the town's skyline, take the lane that passes in front of the county primary school. This goes from the main road at an angle and climbs the slope between some houses. In due course the tarmac road gives way

The Round House, Castle Cary.

to a gravel track and you begin to leave the buildings of the town behind and below. To the left is open grassland, to the right are some handsome detached houses, standing back behind hedges, fences and gardens.

This gravel track is extremely clear, for it leads to a farm. As it curves round to the left so the views open out. At the main group of barns the track turns left, then it passes to the right of a second group and heads for the third and last group, which are straight on and uphill. Upon arriving at that last group of farm buildings – an old piggery and grain tower – you level off, for you will have reached the top of the hill. The views are now all around. Enjoy them at your leisure.

Should you wish to sit down, continue a bit further. Turn left along the side of the piggery and follow the edge of the field along, keeping the fence to your left. At the corner, cross over the stile to the grassy slope. There, upon your right-hand side, is a conveniently positioned bench seat. It faces Glastonbury and, beyond, the Mendip Hills. Down below you is Castle Cary, looking like a miniature model village.

The journey back begins along the ridge of Lodge Hill. Follow the clear path over the grass, keeping the steep slope down to Castle Cary to your left and the trig point to your right. The latter takes the form of a concrete pillar surmounting a grass knoll, the whole mound being fenced off. In due course, you find yourself following a hedge along on your right.

A lovely stretch this – straight ahead on the skyline is the wooded Creech Hill and to the right is King Alfred's Tower. The path is a pleasure to walk along, as it keeps politely to the right of the steep slope down. Soon you come to a gate and stile, a yellow arrow disc nailed up showing the way ahead. Continue into the next field until you reach another bench seat. This is your last chance to sit and enjoy the view. From now on the walk is downhill. In fact, this bench seat overlooks, on the grassy slope way below, the old site of the castle which gave the town its name. The route is by way of these old earthworks. You can either scramble down directly from the bench seat, or you can proceed to the next gate and then turn downhill, to follow the side of the hedge. The latter might be slightly easier.

Very shortly, you will find yourself amongst the old ramparts, the steep banks and deep ditch which once formed the castle's outer defences. It was a Norman castle – thought to have been the fifth largest in Britain at the height of its power. Sadly, it was badly damaged during the 12th century, when it was attacked by King Stephen, and fell into disuse soon after. Now only its site can be made out in the hillside. It is impressive none the less. At the southern end of the ramparts is a deep hollow filled with water. This is Park Pond, the source of the river Cary, used in medieval times for the town's water supply.

In the bottom right-hand corner of the field – at the end of the hedge you have followed downhill – is a stile. This leads to a rough flight of steps and then a tarmac path running down under the trees. Soon you emerge in Castle Cary town centre, opposite the old Market House. Now you could simply turn left and return to the Horse Pond Inn. But you should linger awhile and look round the town itself.

The Market House, supported on columns between which stalls are set up, now contains the town's museum. Inside are local archaeological finds, agricultural and craft tools and various items showing the history of cottage life. During the Middle Ages Castle Cary became famous for spinning and weaving, producing a cloth called Cary Coarse, which was very hard-wearing. Later, sailcloth, linen and rope were also made here.

Behind the Market House, on Bailey Hill and opposite the elegant post office building, is the Round House, also known as the Pepper Pot. This is an old lock-up, built in 1779. It is just 10 ft high and measures 7 ft in diameter, making it Britain's smallest prison. There are only four lock-ups like this in the country.

Other buildings worth seeing, away from the town centre, include the old flax mills in Torbay Road, St Andrews church in neighbouring Ansford, and St John's Priory, at the top of Victoria Road. The last named is an old monastic building that was refashioned into a manor house for John Boyd, the horse hair manufacturer.

Places of interest nearby

The town of *Bruton*, just 3 miles away to the north-east, is an attractive, historic town full of interest. It is almost entirely stone-built. The King's School – the famous educational establishment – now dominates, but other buildings are worthy of note, including the 15th century Priory House, Sexey's Hospital (dating from 1638) and, just outside town, a 15th century dovecote owned by the National Trust.

Hadspen Garden and Nursery (2 miles south-east of Castle Cary) is open four days a week during the summer. This lovely Edwardian garden is a profusion of colour, with roses and herbaceous plants set in an attractive woodland.

Only 4 miles south of Castle Cary are two other attractions – of widely different appeal. The first is *Cadbury Castle*, the fabled site of King Arthur's Camelot. It is a hill fort, occupied intermittently from Neolithic to Saxon times. The ramparts that can still be seen were once topped by elaborate timber fences, making the fortress almost impregnable. Nearby is the *Sparkford Motor Museum*. This was set up by the Haynes Publishing Company and contains vintage and veteran cars and motorcyles. These vehicles are all kept in pristine working order and should be seen.

18 Oakhill
The Oakhill Inn

This pub was created about 100 years ago when two, in a row of three, cottages were converted into an alehouse. In those days Oakhill was not just a farming village but also an industrial one, standing on the edge of the Somerset coalfield. This stretched, in patches, from here to Frome and centred on Radstock and Midsomer Norton, twin towns lying some 5 miles to the north. Across this end of the Mendip Hills the coal seams were largely exploited along the valleys, where they came to the surface. Coal mining well complemented the iron ore mining further west – a long established activity, going back to Roman times.

The Oakhill Inn seems to have shaken off its semi-industrial past. Today it is a most comfortable and sedate establishment. There are carpets throughout, a panelled dado around the walls and a handsome, brick-surround bar. Pictures and plates are hung up and both the wallpaper and the curtains have an oak-leaf motif. It is all very pleasant and welcoming. There are separate rooms and corners – a large public bar, a dining area and a 'snug', the latter used also as a family room.

Opening at normal pub times, this freehouse has an excellent range of drinks on offer, with no less than five real ales (including Royal Wessex and Boddingtons) and Scrumpy Jack cider. The menus are thoughtfully displayed outside, by the lounge door. The snack menu includes sandwiches, salads, ploughman's lunches, pizzas, Welsh rarebit and omelettes. The à la carte menu includes various fish courses (starters and main meals), chicken, steak, duck and lamb. Some of the items are most unusual and tempting, like kidney Gascoigne (with shallots) and fillet of pork in ginger sauce. There are many vegetarian options also, like cashew nut balls in mushroom sauce. All in all, a most impressive line-up.

Telephone: 0749 840442.

How to get there: Oakhill stands up on the Mendip Hills, just 3 miles north of Shepton Mallet. The A367 main road from Shepton Mallet to Bath (which follows the course of the Roman Foss Way) runs through the eastern edge of the village. Frome is 9 miles to the east, Wells is 5 miles to the west. The Oakhill Inn will be found on the right-hand side of the A367 as you come from Shepton Mallet.

Parking: The pub has a large car park. Vehicles can also be left along the main village street (space permitting) but not easily on the A367, owing to the volume of traffic.

Length of the walk: 2½ miles (shorter and longer options). OS Landranger map 183 Yeovil and Frome (inn GR 636473).

The Mendips consist of a high, steep-sided range of hills made of limestone. At their western end the landscape can be fairly barren, with short grass, rocky outcrops, gorges and, underneath, caves. At their eastern end the landscape is slightly more gentle, with wooded combes and well-farmed, rounded hill-slopes. This walk wanders around the latter type of scenery.

The route is mainly along footpaths, which cross fields and run through gates and stiles. The short stretches of country lane used are quiet and very attractive. Throughout, there are views across the surrounding hills. The ground is generally firm underfoot and none of the slopes creates any difficulty

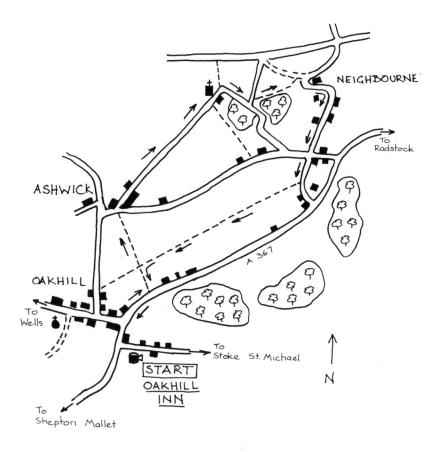

for walkers. Those people pushing prams can enjoy various strolls around Oakhill, keeping solely to the quiet lanes.

The Walk

From the Oakhill Inn walk down the main A367 road northwards. To the left you pass an old Wesleyan church dated 1825 (now converted to industrial use), quickly followed by the gates to Oakhill House. Immediately after these is a 'Public Footpath' signpost, pointing the way up along the edge of the field to the left. This you follow (with the wooden fence on your left-hand side) from one kissing-gate up to another at the top of the slope. Beyond, continue in the same direction, now keeping the hedge to your right and the field – in fact, a playing field with football pitches – to your left. A third kissing-gate at the far end leads onto the road. Turn right.

Be careful at this point, since you join the road at a place where as many as five lanes meet. Take the second on the right. This runs between two houses, the one on the left having a thatched roof and the one on the right having a tiled roof. This lane leads northwards, eventually reaching Ashwick church. At that point the lane suddenly narrows, and road signs announce, for the way ahead, 'Single Track Road' and 'No Through Road'. This, happily, is the direction you take.

Continuing down the lane, now hemmed in by hedgerows, you will see a pleasant panorama opening out ahead. Across the valley are the slopes rising towards Holcombe. As the lane bends right so Neighbourne comes into view, down below.

At the bottom of a sharp little combe, with trees all round, turn left on another lane along the valley. Those wishing to shorten the circular walk, however, should continue straight on – steeply uphill – until they reach a junction. At that point they can turn left then, shortly after, right. This will bring them to the same footpath back that others, doing the full circuit, will later use.

Just 50 yards along the valley bottom lane there is a footpath signpost, pointing the way right. There is a gate and stile here. The next stretch involves a footpath across meadow fields, to the buildings you can see in the distance. You keep to the edge of the first field (with the woodland to your right) and cross the second field to join a track that comes in from your left. Through the next gate you follow that track up, past a farmhouse, to the road. This is a lovely walk, with the hills all round and a scatter of cottages looking down over the green slopes. Neighbourne is little more than a loose-knit hamlet. There is practically nothing to indicate its industrial past.

By following the road uphill, between two houses, the one on the right being called Corner Cottage, you walk through the length of Neighbourne to the top of the hill. Once again, a wider view opens out (this time to the west towards Wells) as you come up from the hairpin bend. In due course you reach a road junction. Go straight on, following the direction signposted to Bath and Shepton Mallet. Those who, earlier, chose to shorten their walk will be joining the route again at this junction.

Ashwick church.

After a couple of hundred yards the lane signposted to Bath and Shepton Mallet bears left. At this point, on the right, you will see a stone stile, set into the hedgerow. This marks the beginning of the last footpath back to Oakhill.

The route is almost dead straight. All the way you will see, or hear, the main A367 road over to your left, since it runs parallel with the path. There are a number of fields to cross, but the way is clear. At each stile the next one to be crossed, in the distance, can be seen.

You follow the edges of the first three fields, first with the hedge to your right, then with the hedge to your left (passing a small barn also). Continue in the same direction, keeping the farm on your left, until you reach a gate. Beyond this you aim for the far corner, where you will find your last stone stile, almost hidden in the hedge. This leads you back to the playing field you skirted at the start of your walk.

The easier, and shorter, way back to the Oakhill Inn is to retrace your original footsteps. Through the kissing-gate this will take you down to the main road where you turn right. Those wishing to take a closer look at Oakhill village, however, should take the longer way back. This leads straight on, keeping the football pitches to your right. At the road north of Oakhill turn left and wander back through the village streets. If you have time, you may wish to look around the little museum, and the local brewery. This would be an apt finale, before returning to the pub where your car is parked.

Places of interest nearby

This being the Mendip Hills, there are numerous archaeological sites to be visited in the vicinity of Oakhill. On *Beacon Hill*, less than 1 mile south, are some Bronze Age burial mounds, marking the site of a cemetery once consisting of more than 17 barrows. There are two Iron Age hill forts nearby – *Maesbury Camp* (1½ miles to the west) and *Blacker's Hill* (2 miles to the north).

Of more recent historical date is *Nunney Castle*, 7 miles to the east, towards Frome. Though badly damaged by Cromwell's troops during the Civil War, this is still a fine example of a small 14th century fortress. It is owned by English Heritage and entry is free.

At Chewton Mendip, 4 miles north-west of Oakhill, is *Priory Farm and Chewton Cheese Dairy*. Here Cheddar cheese is made in the traditional way and guided tours are given in the summer months. In the old Priory gardens are rare breeds of farm animals, picnic sites, a farm shop and restaurant.

The *Ammerdown Nature Trail* will be found near Kilmersdon, 6 miles north-east of Oakhill, south of Radstock. This winds its way up Terry Hill and offers splendid views over the Mendip Hills.

19 Batcombe
The Batcombe Inn

'It's not difficult to find . . . It's damned near impossible!' So runs the pub's advertising slogan. But this refers more to the village than to the pub itself. The Batcombe Inn is, in fact, easy to find once you have found the church – the two buildings stand next to each other. Batcombe village, however, is quite another matter. It is lost amidst the hills and combes of what is, perhaps, the least known part of Somerset.

This attractive, 16th century pub has been extended over recent years to include extra rooms where families can sit and meals can be enjoyed in spacious surroundings. The dining area is pleasantly overlooked by an open gallery-landing, and coffee is served from an airy lobby. The older end of the building has one long bar room with old furniture (note the attractive wooden chairs) and a large, bare stone inglenook where a log fire burns in winter months. The beams have been painted white and decorated with stencils – giving a most pleasing effect.

The Batcombe Inn, which keeps normal pub opening times, is a freehouse. It serves real ale (Wadworth 6X and Butcombe), a huge selection of wines and an interesting range of non-alcoholic drinks (like 'ginger brew', 'elderflower presse' and a herb and fruit concoction). The food is of extremely high quality and people come from miles around especially to eat here. The regular menu, listed on a large card, offers the usual bar snacks together with such succulent main courses as sausage platter, fresh pasta dishes and game. Extra daily specials are also written up on a blackboard, offering delicacies like seafood crêpes, venison burgers, mussels and Parma ham. A cornucopia of food indeed!

Telephone: 0749 850359.

How to get there: Batcombe lies 5 miles south-east of Shepton Mallet and 7 miles south-west of Frome. It is just 3 miles north of Bruton. The village is not served by any main roads, but can most easily be reached from the A359, turning west from Upton Noble. It can also be found by driving eastwards from Evercreech. The inn stands immediately north of the church.

Parking: There is a large pub car park. Vehicles can also be left here and there, around the village, where the width of the lanes permits. Some space is available opposite the church.

Length of the walk: 3 miles (or shorter options). OS Landranger map 183 Yeovil and Frome (inn GR 691391).

This is a most beautiful, undiscovered, corner of Somerset. Clusters of little hills interlock, their green slopes dipping between hidden combes. Fast-flowing streams meander around woodland copses and a network of ancient lanes connects a scattering of farmsteads. Walking anywhere in this area is a delight.

Apart from two short stretches of footpath, at the beginning, this circular walk uses lanes and trackways. It is, therefore, very easy to undertake, and to follow. Many alternative routes present themselves, should people wish to shorten the distance slightly. Those wishing to take just a stroll, or those pushing prams, may simply choose to circumnavigate the village, where there are many attractive old cottages to see.

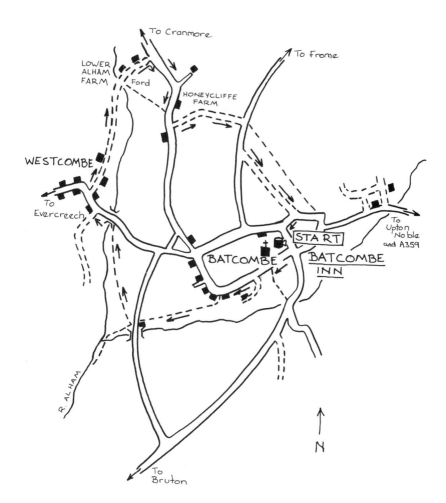

The Walk

From outside the Batcombe Inn turn right, to reach the road junction where stands the church. Those with the time, or inclination, may wish to look round this church before they set off on their walk. It is a lovely, medieval building with some original stained glass, much elaborate carving and, inside, a large amount of Jacobean woodwork. Even those without the time should admire the intricate 15th century tower before they move on.

119

Turning right at the road junction, you proceed westwards, ignoring the track that goes off to the left close to the telephone box. In due course, beyond the cottages on the right, the village lane swings northwards, to run past Boord's Farm on the outside of the bend. Do not follow this bend, unless of course, you intend to shorten the circuit by omitting the two lengths of footpath.

In order to reach the first footpath, turn left immediately before the bend. The way could easily be missed, since it lies through an alleyway, set into a cottage. This cottage forms an archway over the path, upon which is written in stone the date 1793. Walking, in effect, through the cottage, you will find the narrow path runs between gardens to a stile, beyond which is a field. This slopes downhill into a valley, affording you a view beyond, and to the right, of the rolling downland landscape.

Once over the stile you turn right, to follow the top edge of the field for a short while, before going down at an angle to the bottom corner. Aim for the right-hand side of a bungalow, where you will see a gate. Climbing the stile next to this gate, you will find yourself on the road. Cross over, and climb the next stile on the other side.

You now face the second and last stretch of footpath to be followed on this circular walk. But be careful here. There is a footpath signpost, pointing diagonally across the field in a southerly direction (roughly at the same angle as the previous stretch of footpath). Do not follow this route. This path follows the river Alham downstream, towards Spargrove (site of a deserted village and medieval moat). Instead, walk diagonally across the field in a more northerly direction. This path is not shown by the footpath signpost but is certainly a right of way. Soon you meet the river Alham, which you follow upstream, keeping it all the while on your left. This is an extremely pleasant stretch, with the field rising to your right, the sparkling water rushing by and, all around, the green hills looking down.

At the far end a metal farm gate leads onto the road. Turn left and walk uphill, in due course reaching the hamlet of Westcombe. There is a quiet, pretty little road junction here. A war memorial stands in the middle, an old red telephone box huddles close to the wall and, on each side, old cottages look on, across this timeless scene. Turn right here, taking the lane

Batcombe church, with its 15th century tower.

marked as a 'No Through Road' and keeping Wisteria Cottage to your left.

For almost the next mile you follow this lane – and a lovely walk it is, to be sure. It winds about a bit, goes up and down a bit, and offers some wonderful little views all around. The valley of the river Alham is down to your right, the hills of Chesterblade are up to your left. Not far down from Westcombe the tarmac surface changes to stony gravel and earth but it remains firm, dry and clear. There is a hedge on either side. Down in a wooded combe, just a short way along, you pass by a nature reserve run by the Somerset Trust for Nature Conservation. It would be polite not to trespass, so keep to the track.

Later on, and just before Lower Alham Farm, you come to a ford, as the track crosses the valley floor. Wading is not necessary, however. A stile on the left takes you along the edge of a field and then a little footbridge takes you back across the river. Continue up the track, which leads you past the farm and eventually onto the road. Turn right and walk southwards to Honeycliffe Farm. There is, in fact, a right of way that runs across the fields at an angle from the ford to Honeycliffe Farm. It is not very clear and involves some climbing up a grassy slope. The energetic may prefer to use this path and, in so doing, reduce the total length of their walk by some 200 yards!

Continue southwards along the road from Honeycliffe Farm

until you reach a stone house on the right-hand side (called Shankham, although this name is not easily seen, written as it is in the stonework of the façade). Opposite this house is a stony track leading uphill, bounded on either side by a tall hedge. Take this. Halfway up it bends right and continues to another road. Be sure to look back as you climb – the views are superb.

On the road, at the top of the hill, turn right. After about 50 yards you will see a footpath signpost on the left. Those wishing to complete their walk along a path across a field should turn here and follow the direction indicated. Others, content with country lanes and tracks, should continue along the road, keeping the views to the right. The wooded Creech Hill can be seen on the skyline ahead. Very soon there is a stony track leading off to the left. Take this back to Batcombe.

Like others already followed, this wide, gravelly track offers a very pleasant walk, with a hedge on either side and firm ground underfoot. Also, like others, this is probably ancient in origin – Saxon or medieval in date. This particular stretch was once part of the old coaching road to Frome, in constant use in the days before the A359 was built.

Places of interest nearby

The town of *Bruton*, just 3 miles south of Batcombe, is famous for its public school – the King's School, founded in 1519 – but is worth visiting for other reasons. There are numerous old stone houses there, an interesting medieval church with two towers and the 17th century Sexey's Hospital building. Out of town is a 15th century dovecote now owned by the National Trust.

King Alfred's Tower, 4 miles south-east of Batcombe, stands high on the Wiltshire border and commands excellent views all around. It was built in 1772 to commemorate Alfred's victory over the Danes in AD 879. It is said to mark the spot where that great Saxon monarch raised his standard. The tower, which is 164 ft high and contains 121 steps to the top, stands 1,000 ft above sea level.

North-east of Batcombe is the village of *Nunney*, 5 miles away. This boasts a fine example of a Norman castle, once used as a home. Sadly it was badly damaged during the Civil War and is now just a shell.

20 Horsington
The Half Moon Inn

This large stone building, said to date back to the 16th century, does not stand along a main road, so people have to know its existence to find it. But know it they do, because its reputation has spread far and wide. It boasts a wide range of drinks – there are five real ales, including Hook Norton and Lionheart – and the food is excellent. Children are welcome and there is plenty of space for families.

In the front there are two main bar rooms, but these are so interconnected that they could almost be regarded as a single room. One is carpeted, with cushioned chairs and wall seats, the other is more traditionally rustic, with bare floorboards, wooden furniture and, at one end, a large bare stone fireplace. The bar itself has an old-fashioned style brass foot rail. On the walls are numerous pictures of local scenes, some of these being originals and for sale. Beyond these bar rooms is a further dining space and restaurant.

With your real ale, or perhaps with your Taunton Traditional

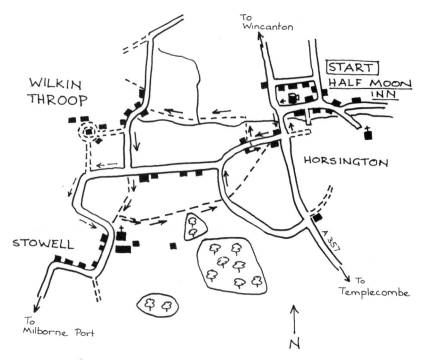

To
Wincanton

WILKIN
THROOP

START
HALF MOON
INN

HORSINGTON

STOWELL

To
Milborne Port

To
Templecombe

A 357

N

draught cider, you can enjoy some good home cooking. Apart from the usual snacks, like rolls and sandwiches, there is a wonderfully inventive main course menu, the daily specials being written up on the blackboard. Starters might include dishes like king prawns in pastry, Cajun chicken wings or moules marinière and main meals could be rabbit with mustard cream and herbs, steak and oyster pie, roast duck with port and orange, 'dynamite drunken beef', or lasagne. The Half Moon Inn is a freehouse. It opens during normal pub times, but longer in summer months.

Telephone: 0963 370140.

How to get there: Horsington will be found in the undulating landscape that rolls between Yeovil and Shaftesbury. Both those towns are 10 miles away, the former to the south-west, the latter to the east. The village stands just off the A357 road, south of Wincanton, 1 mile north of Templecombe. The Half Moon Inn is in the centre of the village.

Parking: There is a large pub car park at the back, and a small area for cars at the front. Vehicles can also be left along the village lanes as it is a quiet place with few traffic problems.

Length of the walk: 2½ miles (shorter and longer options). OS Landranger map 183 Yeovil and Frome (inn GR 702237).

This part of Somerset, close to the Dorset border, is prettily unspoilt and undiscovered. All the landscape is richly farmed, with pasture and arable fields separated by hedgerows, ditches and numerous little streams. There is a scattering of attractive villages and farmsteads and a network of winding country lanes.

This walk takes in two small villages, as well as Horsington itself which can be admired either before or after the circular route. Wilkin Throop and Stowell are hamlets that time seems to have forgotten. Throughout, the walk follows footpaths across farmland. This means that gates, stiles and some wooden fences are encountered, and a few little streams and ditches must be crossed. However, the direction of the route is never in doubt and the ground is firm underfoot.

The Walk

Outside the Half Moon Inn turn right, to go up to the main A357 road, where you turn left. After about 50 yards, having crossed the stream, you turn right along a narrow country lane marked as a 'No Through Road'. A little stone house, called Swiss Cottage, stands at the corner of this lane. By this time you are leaving the village behind and entering the open countryside.

Either before you start this walk, however, or after you have finished it, you should look around Horsington itself. It is a quiet, attractive little place with a number of old cottages. Had you turned left outside the Half Moon Inn you would have come to the duck pond and, close by, an old preaching cross dating from the 13th century. It is thought that this was erected in the time of Edward I when the village was granted royal permission to hold a fair, a market and a court. Up to the right, behind the trees and away from the village is the church, a handsome building looking much older than its Victorian date. Those pushing prams or wheelchairs would enjoy a stroll round the village, and could then take the little lane eastwards to Horsington Marsh, ½ mile away. There they will see the meadows of the river Cale, with its active wildlife, and, crossing the lane, the old course of the Somerset and Dorset Railway line.

Back on the lane running west from Swiss Cottage you soon arrive at some bollards, set in concrete, which block the way to vehicles. These account for the dead-end road sign at the beginning of the lane. Now no longer being used as a motorists' short cut, the route is very quiet and pleasant.

Shortly after the bollards you turn right through a farm gate. This will be seen opposite a house called Combe Mead and just before another house on the right. The path leads down to a river, where you meet a belt of trees. After going through another gate, and actually crossing the river, turn left, taking the path that winds through the woodland and river bank thicket.

This little path brings you up to the open field, where you bear left. The way to Wilkin Throop is now fairly clear, despite the fact that the footpath is not always well trodden. You cross several fields and have to negotiate a number of gates, stiles, ditches and fences. All the while, keep the river over to your left and the open fields rising up to your right. There are two side streams, or tributaries, to cross but these are culverted at the points where the path goes through. The second of the two also has a little wooden bridge. After the first three fields, you should see the houses of Wilkin Throop directly ahead. These give you something to aim for. Many of the fields to be crossed are used for horses and have post-and-rail fencing. Walkers should respect the sensitive nature of these animals.

The last gate, close to some farm buildings, brings you out on the road. This is Wilkin Throop, little more than a hamlet with an adjoining farmstead. But it is very pleasant, with handsome cottages and pretty gardens. The unusual suffix in the name – Throop – derives from the old Saxon word 'throp', meaning 'farmstead'.

Turn left along the road until you reach a T-junction. Here you have three choices. Turn left if you wish to reduce the length of the circuit, this road taking you directly back to Horsington. Turn right if you wish to lengthen the circuit slightly, this road taking you gradually round a wide bend to Stowell church. Go straight on if you want to continue the circuit as originally planned. This will take you by footpath, across a number of fields, directly to Stowell church.

At first the path continues straight on, by some clipped hedges, but after about 100 yards it bears right to cross diagonally over a field to a stile, close to a little copse of trees. You will now see Stowell church – just. It is directly in front, to the right of some farm buildings, but is half-hidden by some trees. The right of way aims for this church, across two fields and through two gates.

Stowell is another tiny settlement, a few houses, a farm and, standing almost alone, a medieval church. The latter was, in fact, originally built for a much bigger village but a combination of the Black Death, in the 14th century, and the spread of sheep grazing in the 17th and 18th centuries, caused the place to shrink in both size and importance. South of the church, on the other side of the railway line, the site of the deserted medieval village can still be seen – in the lumps and bumps of the fields.

The return journey to Horsington, once again, requires the use of a footpath that crosses a number of fields and stiles. Retrace the footpath taken on your way to Stowell church, across the first field, but then veer half-right, to cut across at an angle. The views all around begin to open out along this stretch, especially to the right, towards the Dorset hills. In the distance ahead, about three fields away, you will see a large wood, its dark trees running across the skyline. Aim for the left-hand end of this woodland. The route takes you diagonally across two fields, by way of stiles and a plank bridge over a ditch. As you draw level with the edge of the woodland (by this time over to your right), you will see some houses in front. The path continues in the same direction, this time aiming to the left of those houses. Across the last big field you will see a gate in the far corner. This leads out onto the road.

Once on the road you could, if you wish, continue straight on across another field but this hardly seems necessary. It is easier, and just as pleasant, to turn left and then, after 100 yards, right. This takes you down the little lane with bollards that you walked up at the very start of your walk. Horsington is just a stone's throw away.

Places of interest nearby

Wincanton, less than 4 miles north of Horsington, is a busy little town with much of interest to see. It was once an important stopping point for stage-coaches running between London and the West Country, so there are several ancient coaching inns. The Dolphin dates from 1774, the Red Lion and the Bear are of similar age.

About 5 miles to the west of Horsington is *Cadbury Castle*, a large and impressive Iron Age hill fort. Legend tells us that this was the site of King Arthur's Camelot. A little way beyond this famous archaeological site is Sparkford, home of the *Haynes Motor Museum*. Here vintage and veteran cars and motorbikes are maintained in perfect working order. The display is a 'must' for all vehicle and nostalgia enthusiasts.

Across the border into Dorset are many pretty villages to visit, one of the most attractive being *Sandford Orcas*, 5 miles to the south-west. South of there is the historical town of *Sherborne*, where there are old streets, elegant buildings and, at the edge, the famous castle surrounded by its landscaped parkland.